LAURENCE

THE STONE ANGEL

AND OTHER WORKS

NOTES

COLES EDITORIAL BOARD

Bound to stay open

Publisher's Note

Otabind (Ota-bind). This book has been bound using the patented Otabind process. You can open this book at any page, gently run your finger down the spine, and the pages will lie flat.

ABOUT COLES NOTES

COLES NOTES have been an indispensible aid to students on five continents since 1948.

COLES NOTES are available for a wide range of individual literary works. Clear, concise explanations and insights are provided along with interesting interpretations and evaluations.

Proper use of COLES NOTES will allow the student to pay greater attention to lectures and spend less time taking notes. This will result in a broader understanding of the work being studied and will free the student for increased participation in discussions.

COLES NOTES are an invaluable aid for review and exam preparation as well as an invitation to explore different interpretive paths.

COLES NOTES are written by experts in their fields. It should be noted that any literary judgement expressed herein is just that – the judgement of one school of thought. Interpretations that diverge from, or totally disagree with any criticism may be equally valid.

COLES NOTES are designed to supplement the text and are not intended as a substitute for reading the text itself. Use of the NOTES will serve not only to clarify the work being studied, but should enhance the readers enjoyment of the topic.

ISBN 0-7740-3370-3

© COPYRIGHT 2002 AND PUBLISHED BY
COLES PUBLISHING COMPANY
TORONTO - CANADA
PRINTED IN CANADA

Manufactured by Webcom Limited
Cover finish: Webcom's Exclusive **DURACOAT**

CONTENTS

THE AUTHOR

Margaret Laurence (nee Weymss) was born in the year 1926 in the small town of Neepawa, Manitoba, which is situated one hundred and twenty-five miles northwest of Winnipeg. The area had originally been settled by Scottish pioneers, and in later years the brick houses that they built testified to the prosperity that their Scottish tenacity won from the stubborn prairie. Mrs. Laurence's own family had been among the earliest inhabitants, for her paternal grandfather, John Weymss, was the lawyer who handled the incorporation of the town.

When Margaret was four years old, her mother died. The death of her father came when Margaret was ten. Consequently, she went to live in the big, brick house of her grandfather Simpson, together with her step-mother and a brother. Perhaps some of the emotions of such a move can be captured and understood from a similar situation described in one of her short stories, ''Jericho's Brick Battlements.'' There, following the death of her father, twelve-and-a-half year-old Vanessa has to move with her mother to her grandfather's brick house. The experience is traumatic:

> . . . I watched the man carry in the crates and barrels which held the MacLeod silver and china, and the trunks and cardboard boxes which held our clothes and assorted possessions. Nearly all the furniture had been sold. I wanted the movers to walk slowly, dragging their feet, but they lugged the boxes briskly, joking as though nothing were the matter. I spotted among the other things the suitcase which contained my own treasured objects — a blue glass slipper like Cinderella's, a shiny wooden darning egg, which had been brought from Scotland ages ago and which bore a picture of a town so miniature that you had to use a magnifying glass to see the streets and name — ''Helensburgh, on the Clyde,'' a dozen or so unmatched dangling bead earrings discarded by Aunt Edna, a white silk bookmark which said ''Feed My Sheep,'' in cross-stitch, and the leather-bound telescope which some distant naval MacLeod had once used to sight the enemy. There was a kind of finality about seeing this suitcase of mine going the way of all the other boxes, up the front steps, across the verandah, through the front door of the Brick House. There could be no reversal of decisions now. I felt as though nothing favourable would ever be likely to happen again.

The real-life Margaret needed to have no such apprehensions. Life in the Simpson household was happy, and Margaret's step-mother contributed greatly to that happiness. In particular, Margaret's interest in writing was encouraged by her step-mother. Thus, at the tender age of twelve, Margaret produced her first major work. Written in response

6

to the request of a Sunday School teacher, *Pillars of the Nation* filled two whole school scribblers, and gained for its author an honourable mention in a competition held by the *Winnipeg Free Press.*

In 1944, Margaret left Neepawa to go to university at United College, Winnipeg, where she studied for an honours degree in English. According to anecdotes related by Clara Thomas *(Margaret Laurence. The Canadian Writers Series,* published by McClelland and Stewart), she seems at this period to have been a vital, lively person who brought both maturity and a sense of the unexpected to her relationships.

In 1949, Margaret married Jack Laurence, also a westerner, who was a graduate in civil engineering of the University of Manitoba. Since her husband undertook consulting work for the British government, a period of travelling began. The Laurences moved to England in 1949. Then, in 1950 they travelled to Africa, where Jack Laurence was working on a dam-building project in what was then the British protectorate of Somaliland. Residence in Ghana followed between 1952 and 1957. In this period, both of their children were born: Jocelyn in 1952, and David in 1955. The year 1957 ushered in their return to Canada, and they lived in British Columbia until 1962. The Laurences were divorced in 1969, and Margaret Laurence lived in Buckinghamshire, England.

Margaret Laurence's writing career began in earnest after her move to Africa. Her first published volume was *A Tree of Poverty* (1954), which is a translation of Somali folk tales and poetry. Her first novel, published in 1960, was *This Side Jordan,* which for its plot focused on the tensions of people caught in changing circumstances as the people of Ghana moved towards nationhood. It was given the Canadian Beta Sigma Phi award for the best first novel by a Canadian. *The Prophet's Camel,* also published in the United States under the title *New Wind in a Dry Land,* appeared in 1963, and dealt with the life of Somali nomads. In 1964, *The Tomorrow-Tamer,* a collection of short stories, was published. The first of her major Canadian novels, set in Western Canada, was *The Stone Angel* (1964). The second Canadian novel, *A Jest of God,* was published in 1966. The third was *The Fire-Dwellers,* which appeared in 1969, and in 1974, *The Diviners* was published (this novel is discussed in Coles Notes on *The Diviners*). In addition to the volumes listed, Margaret Laurence has been a prolific writer of articles and short stories, which have been published in many of the leading magazines on both sides of the Atlantic.

Margaret Laurence once declared that a major impulse behind her writing was "to express something that in fact everybody knows but doesn't say or can't express." In her Manawaka stories and novels, there is indeed a vivid focus upon this concern. Perhaps because she was raised in this *milieu* of dour Scottish families, she was familiar with the emotions that lay buried beneath the surface of people's lives. She knew her people well, and the characters she created express their sorrows and their aspirations with poignant force. The family is the dominant unit in what she writes, and the conflicts and tensions, as well as the joys, of the family are portrayed with compassion and accuracy.

LIST OF WORKS

TRANSLATIONS
A Tree for Poverty: Somali Poetry and Prose   1954

TRAVEL
The Prophet's Camel Bell   1963

SHORT STORIES
The Tomorrow Tamer   1964
A Bird in the House   1970

CRITICISM
*Long Drums and Cannons: Nigerian Dramatists
and Novelists 1952-1966*   1968

ESSAYS
Heart of a Stranger   1976

CHILDREN'S STORIES
Jason's Quest   1970
The Olden Days Coat   1979
Six Darn Cows   1979
The Christmas Birthday Story   1980

NOVELS
This Side Jordan   1960
The Stone Angel   1964
A Jest of God   1966
The Fire-Dwellers   1969
The Diviners   1974

CHAPTER SUMMARIES

CHAPTER ONE

Hagar recalled that the stone angel used to stand on the hill above the town, and wondered if it was standing there still, as her father's memorial to "her who relinquished her feeble ghost as I gained my stubborn one."

Her father had told Hagar that the angel was pure white marble and had been brought from Italy at great expense. Hagar now regarded it cynically as a mass-produced product for "fledging pharaohs in an uncouth land."

The angel was the first, the largest and the costliest in the Manawaka cemetery. Hagar remembered the laughter caused by the inscription on one of the lesser angels:

> Rest in peace.
> From toil, surcease.
> Regina Weese.
> 1886

Regina, Hagar reflected, was doubtless forgotten now in Manawaka, just as she herself doubtless was. But Regina deserved her fate. A "gutless creature", she had cared devotedly for an ungrateful mother who, on the death of her daughter, had risen from "sick-smelling sheets" and lived another ten years. No doubt, Hagar thought, she must be "laughing spitefully in hell, while virginal Regina sighs in heaven."

As a girl, Hagar used to walk in the cemetery often, seeking, in her passion for neatness and orderliness, to avoid the wildness of the natural vegetation, which persistently sought to frustrate the efforts of loving relatives to keep the plots "clear and clearly civilized."

Hagar did not usually dwell on the past, for each day now possessed "a rarity." However, for the sake of people like her son, Marvin, she would pretend to be one of those old ladies "feeding ... on the lettuce leaves of other times." She knew she was being unfair in doing this, but carping and smoking cigarettes were now her only pleasures in face of boredom. Though Marvin thought it disgraceful that, at the age of ninety, his mother should smoke cigarettes, Hagar did not care what he or his wife, Doris, thought of her. She had cared too long.

Remembering, Hagar decided not to recall her "lost men." She would not want to be caught crying by "that fat Doris." For the door of Hagar's room had no lock; neither the aged nor the young were granted the privilege of privacy.

Hagar had been, before she started school, a nuisance to her Auntie Doll, a widow who felt that she must live up to the fact that she lived in a big new brick house, the home of Hagar's father, Jason Currie. When Hagar was naughty, Auntie Doll would send her to Jason's store, where her father would make her remember weights and measures. A self-made man who did not believe in wasting words or time, he said little when Hagar's answers were correct. He often reminded his sons, Matt and Dan, that he had "pulled himself up by his bootstraps." The boys, who were graceful and unspirited like their mother, tried to please him but failed. Hagar, who did not want to be like him, had her father's sturdiness, his "hawkish nose", and his intimidating stare.

Mr. Currie mouthed moral homilies and beat his children, most often the boys, with birch switches. When they had had a beating, Matt and Dan used to beat Hagar. She was too frightened to tell her father, but when she learned things about her brothers that they would not like to have repeated, she did inform her father. The boys received a beating which Hagar witnessed.

When her father was getting eggs for a customer, Hagar tried to steal some sultanas from the barrel. She discovered things crawling in them, and announced the fact with glee. Consequently, her father beat her hands with a ruler. Hagar accepted the punishment with dry eyes, and her action bewildered her father, who embraced her and declared that she took after him. In response, Hagar teased him as she ran out of the door, stifling laughter and tears.

Hagar recalled her school friends. There was her best friend, Charlotte Tappen, the doctor's daughter. There was also Lottie Drieser, who did not know who her father was and who was called Lottie No-Name by the boys. Telford Simmons, the undertaker's son, had only "the occasional corpse in the cool vault" to brag about. On one occasion, he sneaked the children into the vault to review the remains of Henry Pearl's sister. Only Lottie had the courage to touch the "small puckered white face."

Hagar was clever at school. Even her father admitted that, and sometimes had to stop himself when on the point of wishing that she had been a boy. Each night Hagar and her brothers would sit in the dining-room doing their homework and listening to their father's advice.

Mr. Currie had come of a good family. His father had been

Sir Daniel Currie, a silk importer who lost his money because of a cheating father. Mr. Currie would make his children recite the name of the family's Highland clan --- Clanranald MacDonald --- their pipe music --- Clanranald's March --- and their war cry, "Gainsay Who Dare!" Because of her father's romantic stories, Hagar thought that Highlanders must be the most fortunate men on the earth, and regretted her father's move to the "bald-headed prairie."

Hagar was about eight years old when the new Presbyterian Church was built. When the minister read out the names of those who had contributed to the new church, Hagar's father bent his head modestly, but he whispered, "I and Luke McVitie must've given the most, as he called our names the first." Hagar hoped the congregation would applaud the list of names, for she had new white gloves, and clapping would show them off.

Though Auntie Doll declared that Mr. Currie was a God-fearing man, Hagar could not imagine his fearing anyone. Her father was, after all, a self-made man. However, he never missed attending a Sunday service, nor saying grace at meals.

Mr. Currie did not marry again, though Aunt Dolly Stonehouse probably fancied he might marry her. She believed that her unattractive appearance held him back, but Hagar and her brothers knew that the real reason for his reluctance was that he could never have brought himself to marry his housekeeper.

Hagar saw her father talking alone with another woman only once. The woman was Lottie Drieser's mother, and Mr. Currie seemed to be trying to persuade her to have intercourse with him. When he was refused, he strode away angrily. She died soon afterwards of consumption, and Hagar's father at that time made three puzzling remarks: first, he expressed sympathy for her troubled life; second, he declared that her sort was not much loss; third, he was startled at the thought that the woman had died of consumption. Hagar was left puzzling which remark was really her father.

Hagar never really knew her brother Matt very well. Skinny and bespectacled, he worked doggedly. He also used to save feverishly the small amounts of money he obtained. Years later, Hagar learned from Aunt Dolly that the money was being saved for Matt's future. However, when he was almost seventeen, Matt must have realized that he would never get enough money to go very far, and he spent all he had on a fighting cock, which was mortally wounded in a contest.

Her brother Daniel was different. Always delicate, he worked reluctantly. Like her father, Hagar thought then that Dan merely "cultivated illness." Daniel died of pneumonia after falling through the ice when skating with the other children. They took him straight home after the accident, and he received his father's admonitions. One night, however, his fever rose. The doctor was away, and Mr. Currie was working late at the store. Matt tried to nurse his brother, and got their mother's old shawl, which he asked Hagar to wear. She wanted to comply, but found herself "unable to bend enough." Consequently, Matt sat for several hours, the shawl draped across his shoulder and Dan's head cradled in his arms, "as though Dan were a child and not a man of eighteen." When Matt returned to the kitchen, Hagar knew that Dan was dead.

When Hagar was almost grown, she was walking past the town dump with her girlfriends when she saw a huge heap of abandoned eggs. With horror, the girls noticed that some of the eggs had hatched in the warm July sun. They could only "gawk and retch" at the sight of the little birds, but Lottie had the courage to deliver the chicks from their plight by killing them. It was the only thing to do, but Hagar knew that she could not have done it, just as she could not bring herself to comfort Dan. Her squeamishness prevented her acting, she supposed.

A timid tapping at the door interrupted Hagar's memories of her childhood. It was Doris, wearing her drab, brown artificial silk dress. Hagar, in contrast, was wearing her dress of lilac silk, which reminded her of the rich lilacs that used to grow beside the front porch of the Shipley place. Doris, "fatly smirking" according to Hagar, had come to invite her downstairs for tea. Irritated, Hagar rose hastily. In her haste she fell, and had to suffer the indignity of Marvin lifting her bulk from the floor. She insisted that they leave the room and then carefully made her own way downstairs.

In the kitchen, Hagar received their attentiveness with suspicion. Her suspicions were confirmed when Marvin revealed that he wanted to sell the house and move into an apartment. The large, four-bedroom house was too big for Doris to look after. Hagar thought of the seventeen years she had spent in this house in this city that had been her home after leaving the prairie, and stubbornly fought the suggestion of selling. Even though she had transferred the house to Marvin when he had taken over her business affairs, she was determined to hang onto the house. In the ensuing altercation, Marvin retired to his den for peace. Unlike Marvin, who valued peace, Hagar was determined. In the truce that followed, Doris prepared to go to church, and invited Hagar to accompany her. When she declined, Doris suggested that the minister should call on Hagar. The old woman complied reluctantly, feeling that "Mr. Troy would be wasting his time in offering … his murmured words."

CHAPTER TWO

Mr. Troy, the minister, chose a bad day to call. Suffering from chronic constipation, Hagar felt bloated, and she found his conversation inconsequential. As he talked, she thought again of the past.

Her father had sent her east for two years to a ladies' finishing school. She had felt that Matt should have been sent to college instead, but, typically, she said nothing of that to Matt. When she returned, she had learned many ladylike things, but nothing to suit her for the life she ultimately led. On her return, Hagar declared that she wanted to teach school. Her father opposed her. They were both "as blunt as bludgeons" in their views. Hagar did not teach; she stayed at home and kept her father's accounts, determined to reimburse him for the two years in the east.

Three years later, Hagar met Bram Shipley, a rough, unsuccessful farmer fourteen years older than herself, whose "fingernails with crescents of ingrown earth" intrigued her. He was, as Lottie Drieser observed, "common as dirt." Perhaps Lottie's words encouraged Hagar's stubbornness. She married Bram against her father's wishes. Matt had married Mavis McVitie the year before, and Mr. Currie and Mr. McVitie had gone halves in building a house for the couple. When Hagar married, neither Mr. Currie nor Matt came to the church. However, she was certain that her father would yield when he saw how Bram "prospered, gentled, learned cravats and grammar." After the reception, given by Charlotte Tappan's mother, Bram took Hagar to the neglected Shipley home. Forgetting that Bram's daughters by his previous marriage had hired out for work whenever they could be spared, she imagined that hired help would soon clean up the place. As soon as they were home, Bram initiated her directly into the mystery of sex. The next day she began to scrub the house out. She had never scrubbed a floor in her life, but she worked that day as though driven by a whip.

Hagar turned her attention once more to Mr. Troy. Hagar listened to his words compliantly, hoping he would soon go. When he left, Hagar felt apprehensive. She wondered what Doris had asked him to mention to her. Her doubts were resolved when she saw the newspaper with an advertisement for an old people's home. She was immediately speared by a pain driving below her ribs. Her aging skin and her hips, which had broadened with age, troubled her. Ignoring

Doris's trivial conversation, Hagar declared that she would not go to the home.

Recovering in the living-room, Hagar glanced over her possessions and wondered how she could leave them: her mother's picture and jug; the gilt-edged mirror from the Currie house; the picture of herself at twenty. As she gazed at the latter, she realized that she was never delicate, handsome perhaps but not delicate. Mavis McVitie had seemed delicate, but she had outlived Matt. Hagar had found his quiet acceptance of death harder to bear than his death itself, and when she had visited Mavis, the widow had spoken strangely: "I never heard him speak harshly of you," she said. "Even when your father talked that way, Matt never did. He didn't dispute what your father said, but he didn't agree either. He'd just not say anything one way or another." A year later, Mavis married a farmer and had the children she had always wanted. After Matt's death, Aunt Dolly thought that Mr. Currie would want to make up with Hagar, but even after the birth of Marvin he did not visit the Shipley home. Perhaps he did not feel that the baby was really his grandson, and Hagar almost felt herself as though Marvin were not her son. Hagar's eyes rested on the plain brown pottery pitcher that had been brought from England by Bram's mother. Hagar did not like it, but Tina did. After all, she was born a Shipley. Hagar hoped that Tina would marry, but wondered where she'd find a man to tolerate her independence. The cut-glass decanter with the silver top had been her wedding gift from Bram. Now, Hagar would not part with it, for it had in the past always been filled with her own choke-cherry wine. The oaken armchair had come from her father's home after a stroke had caused his death. His will had not mentioned the contents of the house, but had specified the money and the property. Some money had gone for the upkeep of the family burial plot, and the rest had been left to the town. Within a month, Currie Memorial Park was started, and beds of petunias 'proclaimed Mr. Currie's immortality.' Even now Hagar detested petunias. It was not that she cared for her own sake or on account of Marvin, but for her son John, who should have gone to college. Jason Currie never saw her second son, or "knew at all that the sort of boy he'd wanted had waited a generation to appear."

Hagar and Doris quarrelled. Hagar dismissed Marvin as a boy who never got upset, even at what happened to his own brother. Doris objected, declaring that Marvin was sixty-four years old and had an ulcer. In the quiet that followed, Hagar asked whether Tina would be home for supper, forgetting that she had left a month ago to take a job down East. Doris and Marvin decided that they must broach the subject of the home. However, at dinner Hagar again became upset when Marvin and Doris mentioned getting a babysitter so that they could go out to a movie. Doris insisted that Hagar needed to have someone with her, because the previous night she had left a cigarette burning and it had fallen out of the ash tray. Marvin and Doris decided not to go to the movie, and Hagar retreated to her room.

In her room, Hagar perused her photographs. She looked at the picture of herself at nine, "a solemn child." There was also her father, "coldly eying the camera, daring it not to do him justice." There was a picture of Marvin the day he started school, dressed in the sailor suit he hated. She had had to give up the idea of dressing Marvin decently, relying on overalls given to her by Bram's daughters, Jess and Gladys. Finally, there was Hagar's picture of John, "a three-year-old standing beside the white cage that held the wren I'd caught for him."

There was no picture of Brampton Shipley. Hagar had never asked him to have one taken, though he was a big, handsome man who wore a beard well. If only he had never opened his mouth! Hagar recalled a visit to Manawaka, when Bram and she had encountered Charlotte Tappen, who had been enthusing over the Glee Club's forthcoming presentation of *The Messiah*. Bram's words to Charlotte had been surly and uncouth: " 'I don't know nothing about it,' he said. 'And what's more, I don't give a good goddam.' " Later, Bram had embarrassed Hagar further in Simlow's Ladies' Wear, by fingering female undergarments and commenting on their price in a loud voice. His reply had been that he did not "give a Christly curse" how he talked. It did not matter to him, he claimed, what her father or her friends thought of him. How simple she must have been, Hagar thought, to believe his words.

Hagar heard footsteps, and thought fearfully that Doris and Marvin had gone out after all, leaving her to the mercy of an intruder. However, the steps were those of Marvin and Doris. At the urging of his wife, Marvin broached the question of the old people's home. Doris, he explained, could not look after Hagar any longer. The care was too much and the lifting too heavy. There were too many disturbed nights. Besides, Doris added, Hagar had wet her bed "nearly every night these past few months." Hagar was appalled at this last revelation. John, she declared defiantly, would not have sent his mother to a home. They would, she warned, be signing her death warrant. However, in the midst of her thundering defiance, Hagar crumbled, and dissolved into tears. The matter was postponed.

Doris helped Hagar to get ready for bed. Sleep came with difficulty. Then the thought of wet sheets jerked her awake, and her feet were seized by cramps. Trying to turn on the light, she knocked the lamp on the floor. The crash brought Doris to the room. When the disturbance had settled, Hagar, alone once more, looked at herself in the mirror. Seeing the "puffed face purpled with veins", the silverish white skin, the dark shadows under the eyes, and the yellow-white hair, Hagar concluded that she was a sight for sore eyes.

She recalled a quarrel she had had with Bram over his ugly habit of blowing his nose with his fingers. It had gone on for years, and nothing she had said changed it. It was obvious that they had both married for the very qualities they later found they could not bear: he for her manners and speech, and she for his indifference to them. And yet, thought of him brought to mind a saying: "His banner over me was love." She had never thought of it as love, finding it hard to connect her romantic concept of love with his sexual activity in bed. His banner over her, she concluded, had been his skin, and now she did not know why it had made her feel ashamed. She had never revealed to him the response which her flesh had made. And now it was too late.

Hagar retired for the night in a bed as cold as winter.

CHAPTER THREE

Waiting for her appointment, Hagar scanned the bare walls of Dr. Corby's waiting-room. There were only two pictures: one of "those weird ones" Tina professed to like, and one of a spring landscape which reminded her of home.

The Shipley place did not have any pictures when she went there, and over the years she managed to put up a few. In particular, Bram never cared for Rosa Bonheur's *The Horse Fair*, declaring that Hagar never cared for real, living horses. She did not admit to him that she was afraid of living horses. In contrast, he was crazy about horses. After a few years of marriage, he had proposed switching from growing wheat to breeding horses. Hagar had opposed him. The wheat was doing well, and she wanted Bram to do well, so that people would be forced to respect him. That night, making love, he had seemed to plead with her to accept his idea, but she had pretended not to understand. He had switched to horses, but had not done well, for he had seemed to be more concerned with finding good homes for the colts than with striking a good deal. When Bram's favourite horse, Soldier, wandered alone into a blizzard and was killed, Hagar had at last admitted the reality of Bram's feelings; she had said, awkwardly, "I'm sorry about it, Bram. I know you were fond of him." But after that night, their emotions had continued to remain unspoken.

Hagar was brought back to reality by Doris's voice asking her to come and sit down. Hagar declared that she only wanted to look at the pictures. The loudness of her voice embarrassed Doris, and Hagar recalled being similarly embarrassed by Bram. In church, during a long sermon, he had whispered loudly: "Won't the saintly bastard ever shut his trap?" Hagar had never returned to church after that. She resolved now to be quiet, though she had never been able to do so before.

Hagar endured Dr. Corby's "coldly intimate touch" during the examination. She was to have X-rays of kidneys, gall bladder and stomach. She was disturbed to learn that she would have to have barium for the X-rays, not knowing what it was.

After supper, Marvin and Doris took Hagar for a drive. She was horrified when they turned into the gates of "Silverthreads", a home for old people. They wanted her to view the place. Hagar tried to resist noticing the comforts of the home and responded gruffly to the "professional benevolence" of the matron. While Marvin and Doris talked to the matron in the office, Hagar sat on the porch, drinking tea. The place reminded her of her first time in hospital, when Marvin was born.

Bram had --- predictably --- driven her right down Main Street when the time came for her to go to the hospital. He had talked enthusiastically of wanting a son, and Hagar had realized with aston-ishment that Bram, like her father, wanted his dynasty. Thus, at a moment when they might have been wishing each other well, she had thought only of his nerve in having such a wish.

On the porch, Hagar was approached by an old woman who complained childishly of the preferential treatment received by another inhabitant of the home. Her place was taken by a second woman, Mrs. Steiner, for whom Hagar felt some liking. Mrs. Steiner's understanding surprised Hagar. She revealed to Hagar that she, too, had not intended to live at the home, but that circumstances had forced the move on her. In reply to Hagar's question whether one ever got used to such a place, she replied with another question: "Do you get used to life?" Upset, Hagar wanted to leave. She found her way to a summer house where, for a brief moment, she thought she saw Bram.

Hagar was taken back to Marvin and Doris's house.

CHAPTER FOUR

It seemed to Hagar that she spent days and days getting the X-rays done. She found the barium nauseating, and resented being strapped in an upright position. At last, she resolved to accept whatever happened and simply wait for what they performed on her.

She seemed to have spent much of her time in waiting. At the Shipley place, she waited, not believing that this could be all her life.

While waiting, she was determined to have a clean house, and filled her time with work. When Marvin was young, she trained him to do chores neatly and promptly, and he used to wait in the kitchen, seemingly seeking her approval.

Bram always had the capacity to leave off work when he felt like it. But after ten years of marriage he did change. He laughed less, and embarrassed Hagar by talking foolishly and ambitiously to the hired hands of his plans for the farm. After harvest, she would see little of him. He would go off drinking with Charlie Bean, and they would return to sleep in the barn, knowing that Hagar would not let them into the house. From Marvin, she would hear the stories of what Bram had done in town. She was particularly horrified when she was told that Bram had urinated on the steps of her father's store. And so twenty-four years had passed in wrangling and bickering. Yet when he turned to her in bed, she would receive him compliantly.

When the doctor's report came, Marvin and Doris seemed to be secretive about the results. Marvin explained to Hagar that there was nothing organically wrong with her; she just needed proper care. However, Marvin was unwilling to pursue the matter of the home again, and Doris decided to invite Mr. Troy again to chat with her mother-in-law.

Sitting in the garden with Mr. Troy, Hagar resisted the bland assurances of the clergyman bluntly. She had never had much use for prayer, she affirmed; it had never seemed to work. He remarked that perhaps she had not prayed for the right things, but her reply was forthright: "If God's a crossword puzzle, or a secret code, it's hardly worth the bother." Further, she observed, she could hardly believe in a merciful God, for she had lost her son, John. The encounter ended awkwardly.

She had not meant to mention John to Mr. Troy. Alone in the garden, she recalled her younger son. The birth had been easy. She had not been anxious over it, as she had been with Marvin. John had proved to be a quick-moving, wiry child, quite unlike the stolid Marvin. Before he started school, Hagar taught him to count to one hundred, and he knew his letters, too. When he was six years old, she told him of his grandfather's ancestry and gave him the Currie plaid-pin. Bram proved to be easygoing with Marvin, but impatient with John, so that even his kindness to the younger boy seemed to have an edge on it. By keeping back some of the money she made from selling eggs, Hagar was able to buy a gramophone and some records. However, John was not much interested in music. In some ways, he showed himself to be "as wild as mustard seed." Once he started school, he began to swear, and he was constantly in fights. Further, he chose "the weirdest crew" as his friends, seeming to resist Hagar's efforts to be a softening influence.

When the First War came, Marvin joined up, though he was only seventeen. As he prepared to leave home, he seemed to seek comfort from Hagar. She found herself unable to give the response he sought. After the war, Marvin did not return home. He went out to the coast and worked at a variety of jobs.

In those days, Bram wore an overcoat that Matt's widow had given to Hagar to cut down for Marvin. Since Matt had been skinny and round-shouldered, the coat did not fit Bram well. One day, Hagar recalled, John came home from school, obviously upset, and told his mother that the children called his father Bram Shitley.

With Marvin's departure, Hagar had to take the eggs herself in order to sell them in town. Unknowingly, she called with John at Lottie's home. Lottie's little girl, who answered the door, was a picture of good grooming. When Lottie herself came to the door, Hagar seemed almost in a trance. Afterwards, she entered the public rest room and looked at herself in the mirror. She saw herself wearing an ill-fitting man's overcoat which bunched and pulled up at the front, for she had put weight on her hips and her stomach since the birth of her children. Her hair was gray and straight, and her face was brown and leathery. Moved by the image in the glass, Hagar decided to get herself new clothes on credit at the store her father had owned. In the store, she found herself pleading for credit, rather than speaking with the aloofness she had intended. Her position became impossible when she discovered that Bram was causing a commotion. He was trying to buy vanilla extract which he could sell at a higher price to the Indians, who used it for drinking. The constable had said that the store was not to sell any more for that purpose. Giving up her plan, Hagar approached Bram, and walked out of the store. That was the last time Bram and she walked anywhere together.

To raise money, Hagar did what she had so far avoided: she sold the things she had from her family home --- her mother's opal earrings, the sterling silver candelabra and the Limoges dishes. She sold them to Lottie, who asked if she was taking a trip. Hagar denied that, but that is exactly what she did do.

Doris's voice burst in upon Hagar as she sat in the garden. After supper, she insisted on accompanying Doris to the store. When they returned, Marvin, as though he had been rehearsing his speech in their absence, announced that arrangements had been made for Hagar to move to the nursing home in one week.

Doris asked whether Hagar would like a sleeping pill, but she refused. Sleep was the last thing she wanted. She was determined not to submit to the home without a struggle. As she lay awake, she tried to recall the name of the quiet place she had picknicked at with Marvin and Doris. It came to her: Shadow Point. She would take her last pension cheque, which Marvin had left lying on the den desk, and go to Shadow Point.

When John was twelve, Hagar had taken him away from Manawaka. She had been determined to leave, even if it meant getting work as a housekeeper, though it seemed a grim joke that now she should think of having the same status as Auntie Doll had had. Bram offered no resistence to their departure. The rail journey was temporarily clouded by John's revelation that he had traded the Currie plaid-pin for a jackknife. However, thinking of the Limoges she had sold, she wondered whether the knife might not be more useful to him after all.

The next morning, Hagar had some trouble in recalling her plan. When she had done so, she saw Doris safely out of the house, took her pension cheque, and headed for the bank. The cheque was cashed without difficulty, and she boarded a bus for Shadow Point. Though she was physically tired, she reached her destination without problems.

At a small store she bought a few provisions: soda buscuits, a tin of greengage jam, a packet of small Swiss cheeses, and some chocolate bars. Leaving the store, she followed a sign saying, 'To the Point'. She had not walked far when a truck driver stopped and gave her a ride. This occurence was fortunate, because her destination, the old fish-cannery road, was three miles further on.

When the truck left, Hagar made her way down the roughly-cut steps to the beach. They were steep and rickety, and Hagar was feeling slightly dizzy. In addition, she was downcast at the sudden realization that she did not have any water with her. Thus, when she reached the bottom of the steps and faced the abandoned cannery buildings, the full weight of her exhaustion seemed to press itself upon her.

Hagar entered an old building in which a manager or owner must have lived, and fell asleep on the thick carpet of dust.

When she awoke, she was hungry and confused, thinking of Doris preparing tea. However, as she became aware of her actual circumstances, she decided she would manage splendidly. She ate some food and then began to explore her new "home."

The house was old and gray, which gave her "a certain reassurance" (perhaps because it reminded her of the Shipley place). The living room was empty of furniture, except for a built-in storage bench, in which she found a pair of old brass weighing scales without weights. The kitchen and the scullery appeared to have been camped in by tramps. In one bedroom there was a brass four-poster bed equipped with a mildewed mattress.

Hagar thought back to Mr. Oatley, for whom she had kept house. He had been good to her and, in return, she had served him well. She had spent her first few months' salary on clothes for John and herself. He had done well in school, in spite of the change. He had seemed to make friends quickly. Though he could not bring them to Mr. Oatley's house, Hagar knew all about them, and she used to enact little fantasies in which she telephoned one of their parents and chatted about the friendship of the boys. Unfortunately, when she did 'phone one mother, Hagar had been informed by the woman that she had no son of that name. Nevertheless, Hagar had not stopped John from "spinning his spiderwebs"; instead, she tried to show him she believed him.

Hagar had sought to encourage John by speaking of the success of his grandfather. Sometimes he would respond enthusiastically, and elaborate on his mother's plans. At other times, he had simply listened to her passively, as though she were humming a lullaby. Their lives had been reasonably content.

In high school, John had made friends, though Hagar had thought them rather "flashy" and suspected them of drinking. John had only smiled at her opinions, for he seemed to have gained "a certain careless confidence from his new height and his handsomeness." He never introduced her to his girlfriends, because he had deceived them into thinking that Mr. Oatley was his uncle. However, the girls had made Hagar sensitive to John's manhood, which she had not cared to dwell on, for it reminded her of Bram's heavy masculinity. There had been times in the night when she would have gone back to Bram, just for the comfort of that masculinity.

Life at Mr. Oatley's had been "a period of waiting and of marking time." And here, she mused, she was waiting once more. She concluded her reflections decisively: "... I can't change what's happened to me in my life, or make what's not occurred take place. But I can't say I like it, or accept it, or believe it's for the best."

CHAPTER SIX

Hagar awoke groggily in the darkness. Rain was driving

through the broken window of the bedroom. She shivered with cold, and her feet were clenched with cramp. The pain under her ribs spread, stimulated perhaps by her fear of being alone.

She recalled her bickering with Doris about the house being cold. What did Doris want? she asked herself. Not money, for Hagar had little of that. Perhaps it was the house she was after; or perhaps Doris just wanted an undisturbed night's rest, which she would get without Hagar. In her confusion, Hagar was sure that they had all left her; she had never left them.

When John was old enough to go to college, Hagar had insufficient money. Consequently, Mr. Oatley got him an office job temporarily. Meanwhile, Hagar saved and invested her money. Unfortunately, the investments turned out badly, and she lost her money. She wanted John to apply for a university bursary, but he refused. It was agreed that he would work for a few years. However, he lost his job, and employment prospects were poor. It was then that he announced that he was returning to Manawaka. Hagar was upset, and just as upset to know that John had written to his father, receiving the reply at Marvin's house. Unwillingly, she let him go as he left to hitch a ride on the railroad to Manawaka.

John's letters were infrequent and said little. In the next two years, Hagar grew stouter. Then John wrote to say that his father was dying, and Hagar returned to Manawaka immediately. She found the prairies in the grip of a crippling drought, so that everyone's farm now looked like the Shipley place. John came to meet her in an old car drawn by a horse. He was dressed in an old pair of Bram's overalls that were stiff with dirt, and he smiled from a face that was like a skull. The interior of the house proved to be just as neglected as the exterior; it had a rancid smell, and the kitchen was a shambles. Hagar was further displeased to note that John had been drinking.

Bram was sitting in the front room. His broadness had gone, and his eyes were absent of expression. Looking at him, Hagar was ashamed of the night thoughts she had had of him during the past years. He did not know her at all. John looked after him completely, "performing all these rites with such zeal and burning laughter they seemed both sinister and absurd." His medicine was home-made potato-wine. When Bram talked, there was only occasional clarity. One day, however, he looked at Hagar with recognition. He declared that she reminded him of Clara --- in Hagar's words, "his fat and cow-like first wife."

John drove Hagar into town to sell the eggs. On the steps of Currie's store, they met Arlene Simmons, Lottie's daughter, who was obviously infatuated with John. Afterwards, Hagar remonstrated with John for his lack of politeness, but he retorted with crude remarks which reminded her of his father.

On another occasion, Hagar met Lottie on the street. Hagar learned that Arlene, now a teacher in the city after having completed university, was home for the summer. Hagar informed Lottie that Bram was dying.

John used to go out after dinner and return at daybreak, a pattern of behaviour that Bram used to follow in past years. She asked about Charlie Bean, Bram's former drinking companion, and learned that he had been dead for years. She declared that that was 'good riddance to bad rubbish', but was puzzled when John spoke of Charlie having given him jellybeans and sleigh rides when John was a child. Hagar concluded that they must be "remembering two different men." John also revealed to whom he had traded the Currie plaid-pin for a knife. He no longer had the knife; it had not been much of a knife, and he had sold it to buy cigarettes. Hagar sadly recalled the family motto: "Gainsay Who Dare."

One day, Hagar got John to drive her to the cemetery. The Currie family plot was still cared for, but, to her horror, she found that the stone angel had been toppled. She insisted that John set it upright again. She was horrified again to discover that someone had painted the angel's lips with lipstick. As she erased the smear, John said that he did not know who had done it, but she did not believe him.

Marvin came to Manawaka, but only stayed a few days. He and John bickered constantly. Marvin wanted John to return to the coast to find work, but he insisted that he was better off on the farm, for he could obtain welfare money. Angrily, Marvin pointed out that manual work was available, and reminded his brother that he had left home at seventeen to go to war, and had had a variety of heavy jobs after that. As Hagar listened, she wanted to ask Marvin about his taxing experiences, but she could not bring herself to do so. John replied defiantly that he was through with living in other people's houses.

Bram did not recognize Marvin, even though Hagar heard him enter his father's room one night and whisper that he was sorry. Hagar did not know why, but she wanted to say to Bram what Marvin had said. However, she concluded that there was nothing she could do for him now.

Bram died in the night. Marvin sent money to help with the expenses, and also sent word of the birth of Christina. Bram's daughters did not attend the funeral, but did come to the farm to collect some things that had belonged to their mother. They did say, however, that their father should be buried as close to their mother as possible. Hagar did otherwise. She had the Shipley name added to the side of the Currie gravestone, and Bram's body was interred in the Currie family plot. She was worried whether she had done the right thing, but John assured her that it did not matter, for "They're only different sides of the same coin, anyway, he and the Curries. They might as well be together there." After the funeral, it was John who cried, not Hagar.

CHAPTER SEVEN

The sun woke Hagar and, as she examined her plight, she was tempted to return to Marvin and Doris. However, as she thought of the home to which she would be sent, she resolved to struggle on, and went out in search of water. She discovered a rusty and dinted bucket, from which sparrows were drinking rain water. She shooed the birds away and drank.

On the beach, she saw two children playing --- a boy and a girl, both about six years of age. They were playing house, but were quarrelling in the process, because the girl was being domineering. Hagar wanted to warn the girl that she would lose her friend. When Hagar did speak, the children were frightened. They left quickly. Hagar regretted her action. Of course the children would be frightened at the sudden sight of "a fat old woman" with "a beckoning leer."

Hagar decided to eat, but the food was tasteless to her. Then she remembered that she had not moved her bowels that day. She wended her way back to the forest on the hill and sought a quiet place. She was unsuccessful in her efforts to defecate. As she sat in the forest, the setting seemed to suggest a courtroom in which she was being tried. Then she grew weary of the game. She was just like the children playing house, and remembered other children who had played house, though somewhat differently.

When Bram died, Hagar informed Mr. Oatley of the death, and he agreed that she should stay in Manawaka a few weeks more.

Cleaning the attic, Hagar found some things that had belonged to Clara, Bram's first wife: a bookmark for a Bible, and a little gold ring, which had in the centre a coil of hair from Bram's firstborn child who had died. Hagar decided to take the things to Bram's daughter, Jess. She found John at Jess's. Unobserved, she listened to their conversation. John was asking about his father. As she listened, Hagar was annoyed by the intimacy between the two. She entered the house and gave the little box with Clara's keepsakes to Jess, though she did not want Bram's daughter to regard it as any kind of peace offering. John followed Hagar home with "mock-meekness".

Hagar did not know that John was going out with Arlene until she brought him home drunk on one occasion. The next day, John did not even remember that it was Arlene who had brought him home. He had got into a fight at a dance, which Lottie and her husband had also attended. Hagar was horrified, and was sure that Arlene's bringing him home had been a mocking gesture, "flaunting him like a ragged flag." To John, however, Arlene's gesture had different significance. To him, it was a sign that she really did care for him.

Hagar had to return to the coast, but the following summer she went back to Manawaka for the summer. Noticing that the house had been cleaned, she was informed that Arlene was responsible. She visited often, because she no longer had her job and was staying with her parents, who were also experiencing the difficulties everyone was facing in the economically troubled times. To Hagar, Arlene did not look so pretty as she had been, and she dressed more plainly. In a conversation with Hagar, she revealed that she was in love with John and wanted to marry him. Hagar poured scorn on the idea. They had no money, she declared, and John was a hobo who drank too much. Arlene, she warned, should not think of marrying him with the idea of changing him. Arlene retorted that Hagar did not know John.

That night, Hagar remonstrated with her son over the relationship with Arlene. The Simmons' family, she affirmed, were "nothing to write home about." When Telford was a boy, she continued, his mother had done ironing to make extra money. John insisted that the relationship was no concern of Hagar's. She retired for the night, leaving him sitting in the darkness. It helped him to think, he said. In contrast, Hagar feared the darkness; for her, "it teemed with phantoms, soul-parasites with feathery fingers, the voices of trolls, and pale inconstant fires like the flicker of an eye."

One sultry afternoon, as Hagar lay half-asleep in the front room, John and Arlene came home. They thought that Hagar was out, and they began to discuss their situation. Arlene wanted to get married and to bear a child of John's. He was more cautious, and said that they could get married when his mother returned to the coast. Their talk ended in love-making and, as she listened, Hagar found it incredible that "such a spate of unapologetic life should flourish in this mean and crabbed world." Afterwards, Hagar fumed as she thought of what Lottie would think of the situation, and she resented the love-making in her house. She waited impatiently as John and Arlene enjoyed a meal together and then finally went out. Hagar went to bed to make her plans.

The next day, Hagar discussed the situation with Lottie. For a while, the two women traded veiled insults. However, it was finally agreed that it would be a good idea for Arlene to leave Manawaka for a while. Lottie would arrange for Caroline, Telford's cousin down east, to invite Arlene for a visit. Thus, the two women reached agreement, "no longer haggling with one another, but only with fate, pitting our wits against God's."

A month passed. Arlene visited constantly, until at last Hagar objected. John did not bring Arlene to the house again during the following month.

Hagar came to herself with a start. She decided that she could not return to the old house where she had stayed. The stairs were too much for her, and she feared intruders. She would move to the cannery building.

CHAPTER EIGHT

To Hagar, the cannery building seemed to be a place of "remnants and oddities." An enormous room with high rafters, it was strewn with rusted machinery, old rope, wooden boxes and discarded fishing nets. At the far end stood a derelict fishboat, looking as though it "might have been washed up somewhere centuries after it had set out for heaven with its Viking dead."

As she used boxes for a chair and table, Hagar reflected that she had all she needed. After eating, she noticed a number of dead June bugs. She plucked the artificial flowers from her hat and replaced them with the bugs in her hair. She was pleased with the new jade and copper pieces.

Suddenly she felt worn out. The pain in her chest could not be ignored, and her feet were swollen. She could not remember what she had done that day. She slipped to the floor in a swoon.

A sea gull flew into the room. Hagar remembered the old saying that a sea gull meant death if it flew into a house. Desperately, she thought that Marvin would know what to do with the flying bird. At last, she flung a wooden box at it, injuring its wing. It dragged itself to a pile of nets and lay, "throbbing aloud."

In the darkness, feeling that all about her was "distorted" and "haggard", Hagar sang a hymn, "Abide with Me." Suddenly, she heard outside the barking and snarling of dogs. Then the door opened. A man as frightened as she was stood there and struck a match. She thought at first that it was someone Marvin had sent to take her home. It was not. The man was Murray Ferney Lees, a salesman for Dependable Life Assurance. He lighted a candle and pulled a jug of red wine out of a paper bag. As the two relaxed under the influence of the wine, he told Hagar his life story. His mother had been Anglican and his father United Church. However, under the influence of his grandfather, he had joined the evangelical Advocates. He had met his wife, Lou, a woman with "great white thighs", at Bible camp, and had been crazy about her. Lou had become pregnant before they were married. She had intended to tell everyone that the baby was premature, but when it was born it weighed nine pounds twelve ounces. The deception was impossible, and Lou had regarded it as a sign of God's punishment. She had become half-hearted in sex, but redoubled her efforts at the Tabernacle. Murray's faith had wavered, especially in view of Lou's judgement of their son, Donnie. And then a preacher at the Tabernacle had announced the end of the world. The preacher, a member of the Redeemer's Advocates, had conducted vigil meetings at the Tabernacle. At one of the meetings, Murray had decided that he had had enough. He left for home. When he got there, he found, to his horror, that his house had burned down: Donnie, left alone at home, was dead.

Hagar did not know what to say to Murray. She murmured that she, too, had lost a son. In the silence which followed, they both seemed to sit waiting for "the terrible laughter of God", but all they could hear was "the vapid chuckling of the sea".

Murray could not decide whose fault it had all been: his grandfather's for being a "Bible puncher", his mother's, whose behaviour had driven him to evangelical religion, his wife's, who had assured him that Donnie was safe, or his own, for having gone to the vigil meeting in spite of the fact that he felt it was not doing him any good. Now, he said, his wife had told him he had the perfect excuse for his behaviour. Perhaps, he reflected, after five years that's all it was, an excuse. Hagar and her strange companion settled down to sleep.

Hagar recalled that John had told her that Arlene was moving east for a year. Her father's cousin was going to pay her for helping in the house. He suspected for a moment that Hagar knew already of the arrangement, and said defiantly that he would get Arlene pregnant before she left. Hagar replied that she had only wanted the best for him, and he retorted that she had "always bet on the wrong horse", for Marvin was really her boy, and she had never seen that. But he never brought Arlene back to the Shipley place again.

That night, before he left to go out as usual, they quarrelled over Arlene. Later, Henry Pearl came to the door. John was in hospital; he had had an accident. John, drunk at a dance, had accepted a bet that he could drive his truck across the railroad trestle bridge. However, an unscheduled freight train had arrived and struck the vehicle. Arlene had been killed instantly. In the hospital, John cried out in pain, asking his mother for help. Before she could speak or move, he observed harshly that she could not help. And then he died.

Hagar stiffened her spine, so that she would not cry in front of strangers at the hospital. When she arrived home, however, she discovered she could not cry. She felt as though she were "transformed to stone." She had only one thought: that there had been so many things to be said to John and so many things to put right, but he had not waited to hear. After the funeral service, she would not go to the cemetery.

She attempted to talk to Lottie, but Lottie was too ill. Hagar envied her the comforting presence of Telford.

Afterwards, Hagar sent everything of value in the house to Marvin, and sold the home. She returned to Mr. Oatley's.

The following year, Mr. Oatley died and left Hagar ten thousand dollars in his will. She bought a house with the money.

As she remembered, she wept. Murray sought to comfort her, but she insisted that John's death had been senseless, and she would be angry over it until she died. In response to her pleading, he did not leave her, and they both settled down to sleep once more.

Hagar awoke and vomited. Confusing him with John, Hagar assured him that she was alright. Murray settled her down so that she could sleep again.

Chapter Nine

In the morning, Hagar awoke, stiff with cramp. Her companion had gone, but before leaving he had covered her with his coat. Now she could hardly believe that she, "always fastidious if nothing else", had drunk with a perfect stanger and slept huddled beside him. In her confusion, she knew that important words had been spoken the night before, but she could not remember what they were. Also, she felt as though she had been recently bereaved; why, she did not know.

Suddenly, Marvin and Doris appeared, brought by Murray Lees. In her heart, Hagar was relieved to see Marvin, though she despised her own weakness in rejoicing at being captured. However, characteristically she rejected the help of Doris, who then reminded her that Mr. Lees had saved her life. At that moment Hagar remembered something of the previous evening and apologized to Lees. As he left, Hagar experienced a feeling that it was a "kind of mercy" that she had encountered him.

In the car, Marvin assured Hagar that there was now no question of her going to the old people's home. The X-rays had revealed a serious illness, and Hagar would have to go to hospital. She was both repelled and stunned at the news. Only now could she see that what was going to happen could not be delayed indefinitely.

In hospital, Hagar lay in the public ward, because Marvin had been unable to obtain other accommodation. She felt like "an exhibition in a museum." She resented the patronizing jollity of the nurses, and caused difficulties over taking her medication. Under the influence of a pain-killer and a sleeping pill, she drifted off to sleep as the pain gradually waned.

A different nurse, who seemed to be less condescending than the other, wakened Hagar and gave her another pill for the pain. Touched by the nurse's sympathy, Hagar wept.

The woman in the next bed, Elva Jardine, prattled endlessly. She woke the other two in the room, the mountainous Mrs. Reilly, and Mrs. Dobereiner, asking them to support her statement that Hagar had talked constantly in her sleep. Hagar got rid of Mrs. Jardine's attentions by being rude to her and then, aided by more of the soothing pills, she settled into a "hazy lethargy."

Marvin visited Hagar. She did not mean to complain, for she was pleased to see him, but when she spoke a string of complaints came from her. She grumbled at the accommodation, at the nightclothes she was forced to wear, and at the bland diet she was receiving. She knew she was being unreasonable, but she could not stop. She always had to find who was to blame. When Marvin left, assuring her that he would try to obtain semi-private accommodation for her, Hagar felt ashamed, for she knew that Doris was unwell.

Mrs. Reilly's husband, Tom, was visiting his wife. Their talk had such tenderness that Hagar was ashamed to be listening. When he left, Mrs. Reilly's meek surrender to not having bread with her meals enraged Hagar. In her place, Hagar observed, "I'd roar for bread until I was hoarse, and die of apoplexy if I pleased." Her thoughts were interrupted by Mrs. Dobereiner's request for the bed pan. Mrs. Jardine announced that she was going to the bathroom by herself. When Mrs. Jardine had left the room, the nurse told Hagar that Mrs. Jardine would not be leaving for some time; she had only one operation, and had two more to come. Hagar refused the offer of a bed pan, saying she could get to the bathroom by herself. The nurse informed her that she was not to get out of bed.

When Mrs. Jardine returned, Hagar learned that Mrs. Dobereiner's words in German were in part a prayer for death. Mrs. Jardine also revealed that Mrs. Reilly prayed a great deal. It was then that Mrs. Jardine revealed that her husband and she were from Freehold, only twenty-five miles from Manawaka, and that they knew the Pearl family. Hagar warmed to Mrs. Jardine's kindly interest.

Pain prevented sleep for Hagar. The nurse would not give her a hypo without the doctor's instructions, and Hagar was given another pill. She apologized to the nurse for her previous rudeness.

In the night, Hagar alarmed Mrs. Jardine by trying to reach the bathroom on her own. The nurse came to get her back to bed, seeking to give her assuring by pointing out that it was Hagar's right now to receive help. In bed once more, she drifted off to sleep.

When the doctor visited the next day, Hagar asked for a hypo when she needed it. He agreed readily. Then Marvin and Doris visited. Hagar felt her old contempt for Doris, thinking how ridiculous Doris's hat looked with its burden of artificial flowers. When Doris told Hagar that Tina was going to be married to a young lawyer, Hagar rebuked Doris's cautious approval of the marriage. Then, pulling her mother's sapphire ring off her finger, Hagar told Doris to give it to Tina. Hagar was further distressed at the news that she was to be moved to a semi-private room. She spoke snappishly to her son and daughter-in-law, and they left.

A large trolley arrived to move Hagar to the semi-private room.

CHAPTER TEN

Worried at the cost, Hagar lay in her semi-private room. Her nurse proved to be a pretty, slender girl no more than twenty. Hagar felt flattered when the girl told her that she was still handsome. The girl sought to cheer Hagar up, telling Hagar that she was lucky, for she had all the years behind her that nothing could take away. But Hagar felt a troubled evasiveness behind the girl's words, and wondered what it was that had taken the pleasantness from the conversation.

In the night, Hagar, half asleep, left her bed. She was making for a light, confident that if she reached it Bram would call her name. A nurse led her back to bed and insisted on dressing her in a restraining jacket. Hagar objected, and then yielded before the nurse's desperation. Hagar apologized to the nurse for the trouble.

When Hagar awoke, the other bed was occupied by a sixteen-year-old girl, Sandra Wong, who was to have an appendectomy. She was worried over the operation, and Hagar reassured her, falsely saying that she had had her appendix out years ago and it was not a serious operation. As they talked, Hagar felt the distance of age between them.

The next day went slowly. Sandra was recovering from her operation, and Hagar drifted in and out of a drugged sleep. She was awakened by Doris, who had brought Mr. Troy. She left him alone with Hagar, who felt almost sorry for him because he was perspiring so much. In spite of Hagar's indifference, he tried to pray. Then Hagar interrupted his praying with a request that he sing a hymn. The fumbling of his prayers gone, he sang "All people that on earth do dwell" firmly and surely. Hagar was deeply affected as the last line rang out: "Come ye before Him and rejoice." She knew then that she had wanted to rejoice all her life, but had been held back by "some brake of proper appearances". Pride had been her "wilderness" and fear had been the demon which led her. She thought of Bram and John, both dead, and wondered whether they were dead by their own hands or by hers. Hagar wept, and her tears disturbed Mr. Troy. He thought his visit had failed. She wanted to reassure him, but she could not find the words. When Doris returned, Hagar could not prevent herself from being snappy. Thinking herself "unchangeable" and "unregenerate", Hagar sought to assure Doris that she had actually enjoyed Mr. Troy's visit, but Doris was unbelieving.

Later, Hagar was visited by her grandson, Steven. He revealed that Tina was to be married down East. Doris was going to fly down for the wedding. The date was undecided, and Hagar realized that the arrangements were dependent upon her death. As they talked further, Steven reminded her of how she used to give him 'jaw-breakers' when he was a child. She realized that that was all she was to him --- "a grandmother who gave him money for candy." The weight of all the "incommunicable years" pressed upon her, and she could not find the right words to utter. When she asked him if he was really alright, he seemed startled, and she realized that he was troubled by things she did not know about. However, she could not take on extra burdens now. Before he left he kissed her. She would have liked to have told him how dear he was to her, but she would only have embarrassed both herself and him.

The visit ended, and Hagar, discomforted by pain, sought the needle greedily once more. When she awoke, Sandra was feeling pain and rebuked Hagar for her previous assurances. In reply, Hagar was blunt. Sandra asked the nurse whether she had to stay with Hagar. The nurse whispered to the girl, obviously informing her that Hagar was dying. The girl was distressed. She was evidently wondering, with fear, what would happen if Hagar died in the night.

In the night, Hagar was annoyed at being awakened by the sounds made by Sandra. She wanted to go to the bathroom, and the nurse had not answered her call. Hagar put the light on to comfort the girl, who continued to be distressed by her need. Hagar felt sorry for her. She should not, Hagar thought, have to suffer such pain and humiliation at her age. At last, Hagar decided. She would get the bed pan for the girl. Ponderously and painfully, she made her way to the bathroom. She had just obtained the bedpan for the girl when a nurse arrived. Hagar was bundled back into bed. When they were alone once more, Sandra began to laugh at the nurse's astonishment and concern. Hagar joined in the laughter, and both of them bellowed and wheezed with their painful laughter. Then they slept peacefully.

In the days that followed, Hagar had confused awareness of Sandra's concern for her. She came over to the bed often, bringing a drink of water or pulling the curtains when Hagar wanted to sleep. On one occasion she dabbed Hagar's wrists with cologne.

Marvin came. Unable to understand what came over her, Hagar confessed that she was frightened. Marvin apologized for any harsh things he had said over the years. He reached for her hand and held it tightly. She thought then of asking his pardon, but she knew that that was not what he wanted at that moment. Instead, she assured him that he had been a better son than John. It was a lie, but Marvin believed her. As he left, the nurse remarked on Hagar's strong constitution. He replied that his mother was a holy terror. On hearing these words, Hagar felt that she had got more out of life than she could have reasonably expected, for Marvin had spoken with "such anger and such tenderness."

Hagar recalled the last time she had visited Manawaka, on a trip with Marvin and Doris. The Shipley place had vanished, replaced by a smart new house and a new barn. At the cemetery the angel was still standing. A young caretaker, not knowing them, spoke enthusiastically about the cemetery. He pointed to the unusual stone bearing the two names of Currie and Shipley. They were two of the earliest pioneering families in the district, he declared. And so, Hagar thought, both families were at last the same. "Nothing to pick and choose between them now. That was as it should be."

Hagar lay in her "cocoon", "woven around with threads" and "held tightly", with young nurses coming to loosen her bonds with the soothing needle. Sandra appeared to announce joyfully that she could go home in a few days. When she went away, Hagar tried to recall something "truly free" that she had done in her ninety years. There were only two things, she concluded, and they were both recent. One was a joke, and the other was a lie. And yet it had not really been a lie, "for it was spoken at least and at last with what may perhaps be a kind of love."

As the pain increased, Hagar asked impatiently for the needle. She also asked crossly for Doris to help. Doris brought a glass of water, which Hagar insisted angrily on holding herself.

And then she died.

REVIEW QUESTIONS

CHAPTER ONE

1. Give an account of the Shipley stone angel.
2. Describe the personality of Mr. Currie, as it is revealed in Chapter one.
3. Describe Hagar's personality as a child.
4. Describe the history of the Currie family.
5. What were the three puzzling remarks Mr. Currie made after the death of Lottie's mother? Why do you think that they puzzled Hagar so much?
6. Compare and contrast the personalities of Hagar's two brothers.
7. Describe Marvin and Doris. Is Hagar's irritation with them justified?

CHAPTER TWO

1. What does Hagar's attitude towards going to school in the East reveal about her character?
2. Describe Bram Shipley. Why was Hagar so attracted to him?
3. Give an account of Hagar's relationship with her brother, Matt.
4. Why did Hagar detest petunias so much?
5. Explain the reasons why Marvin and Doris want Hagar to go to a home.

CHAPTER THREE

1. What did Bram's affection for horses reveal about (a) Bram and (b) Hagar?
2. Give an account of Hagar's visit to the home.

CHAPTER FOUR

1. Give an account of Hagar's relationship with (a) Marvin and (b) John.
2. Explain the importance of Hagar's chance encounter with Lottie and her daughter.
3. What does Hagar's conversation with Mr. Troy reveal of her view of life?

CHAPTER FIVE

1. Describe (a) Hagar's flight to the coast with John and (b) her escape from Marvin and Doris.
2. Describe the outside of the house Hagar stayed in at the shore. What possible symbolic significance did the house have?
3. What surprising item did Hagar discover in the storage bench in the living room? Of what possible significance was it?
4. Describe John's behaviour while he lived with his mother at Mr. Oatley's.

CHAPTER SIX

1. Give an account of the circumstances which led to John's return to Manawaka?
2. Explain the details which emphasize John's growing likeness to his father.
3. Who had possibly toppled the stone angel in the cemetery? Relate this action to Bram's behaviour at Currie's store, in chapter four.
4. Describe the effects which Marvin's visit to Manawaka had upon Hagar.

CHAPTER SEVEN

1. What relevance to her own life did Hagar find when she observed the children playing on the beach?
2. Explain the different interpretations Hagar and John had of Arlene's attitude in driving John home after the dance.
3. Describe Hagar's conflicting emotions when she overheard John and Arlene making love.

CHAPTER EIGHT

1. Describe Murray Lees appearance, and give an account of the experience which had brought him sorrow.
2. Give an account of the similarities between Hagar and Murray Lees.
3. Describe the circumstances which led to the deaths of John and Arlene.
4. With whom did Hagar confuse Murray Lees at the end of the chapter? Why did his words bring her such comfort?

CHAPTER NINE

1. Give an account of Hagar's early behaviour in the hospital.

Describe the indications of a softening in her behaviour towards the end of the chapter.
2. Account for the change in Hagar's behaviour.

CHAPTER TEN

1. Describe the fluctuations in the relationship between Hagar and Sandra Wong.
2. Describe Mr. Troy's visit to Hagar. What important revelation had the visit brought to Hagar?
3. Give an account of the visit of Steven. What did Hagar learn from that visit?
4. Give an account of Marvin's last visit to his mother.
5. What was the joke Hagar had enjoyed? What was the lie she had told? Why did she regard them as significant?

CHARACTERS

HAGAR SHIPLEY

In *Survival*, "A Thematic Guide to Canadian Literature", Margaret Atwood mentions Robert Graves' three mythological categories for women: first, Diana, the young girl; second, Venus, goddess of love, sex and fertility; and third, the Crone, goddess of the underworld, and associated with death and oracular powers. Miss Atwood wonders why there is such a predominance in Canadian literature of Hecate-Crone figures, and declares later that Hagar Shipley in *The Stone Angel* is "the most extended portrait of the frozen old woman."

There is much truth in Miss Atwood's judgement of Hagar. Born the daughter of Jason Currie, a strong, unyielding, self-made man, she inherited her father's harsh qualities. She possessed a "stare that could meet anyone's without blinking an eyelash" (p. 8), and to others revealed a flinty heart that rivalled that of the stone angel in the Manawaka cemetery. Such was the strength of her self-control that those around her received no hint of the passions that seethed below the icy surface. Typically, for example, she did not weep at the death of her husband or at the death of her beloved son, John. Her heart was moved often, but her tongue, firmly ruled by her unbending pride, gave no expression to the passion that she felt. At times in her strange relationship with Bram, she felt for him an emotion close to love, as when she felt his sorrow over the death of his favourite horse, or when she felt the warmth of the physical love that he offered her, but she resisted all notion of giving voice to the emotion that welled within her. She regarded such expression as "betrayal", to be resisted and tamed.

Her frozen exterior was the result of the inheritance of pride she had received from her father, a pride that feared any weakening of her status. For this reason, she despised weakness in any form. Thus, she had nothing but scorn for the dead Regina Weese whose body lay in the Manawaka cemetery, because Regina had been "a flimsy, gutless creature, bland as egg custard, caring with martyred devotion for an ungrateful fox-voiced mother year in and year out" (p. 4). There was no thought for, or appreciation of, the apparently selfless love that Regina had shown. Further, Hagar even despised her own dead mother, dismissing her as "that meek woman". Over-zealous attention to the past glories of the Currie name led her astray, and led her into contemptuous judgements of others: "Telford's father wasn't very highly regarded" (p. 11); Aunty Doll was "such a homely woman with her sallow skin" (p. 17); her brother Daniel "was always delicate, and he knew very well the advantages of poor health" (p. 21); Lottie was "light as an eggshell" and Hagar "felt surly towards her littleness and pale fine hair" (p. 27); Doris is said to speak with a "whispery whine" (p. 28); Mr. Troy is rather "a stupid man" (p. 55); Murray Lees is judged to be "rather a coarse man" (p. 227); Mrs. Jardine is a "tiny crone" with "hidden malice" (p. 259). The catalogue of Hagar's adverse judgements could be longer, for she had an unerring eye for the worst in others who felt the lash of her withering scorn or condescending pity.

With such an attitude, it is scarcely surprising that Hagar brought nothing positive into the lives of those around her. The list of her crimes is lengthy:

--- She was unable to grant to her dying brother, Daniel, the comfort that Matt gave

--- She failed to voice her concern for Matt's ambitions and aspirations when she, and not Matt, was sent East

--- She married Bram Shipley in a spirit of wilful pride and self-sufficiency, thereby alienating her father

--- She entered into marriage with Bram in the expectation of changing him into the image of what she thought he should be, and deliberately denied him that affection and sharing which might have made him less rebellious and despairing

--- She denied her own son, Marvin, the love that he sought as a child, impatiently dismissing his slowness of speech and lack of natural charm

--- She sought to rule the life of her son, John, trying to fashion him in the image that was desirable to her, and in the end interfered in the love between Arlene and John, with disastrous consequences.

Her own judgement of herself is a true one:

... I must always, always, have wanted that - simply to rejoice. How is it I never could? I know, I know. How long have I known? Or have I always known, in some far crevice of my heart, some cave too deeply buried, too concealed? Every good joy I might have held, in my man or any child of mine or even the plain light of morning, of walking the earth, all were forced to a standstill by some brake of proper appearances - oh, proper to whom? When did I speak the heart's truth?

Pride was my wilderness, and the demon that led me there was fear. I was alone, never anything else, and never free, for I carried my chains within me, and they spread out from me and shackled all I touched. Oh, my two, my dead. Dead by your own hands or by mine?

(p. 292)

There are, therefore, in the novel two images for Hagar which illustrate her nature and her predicament clearly. One image is that of the stone angel in the Manawaka cemetery (see SYMBOLS AND IMAGES). Hagar *is* the stone angel in that, first of all, it suggests a hardness and a lack of feeling which are characteristic of Hagar, and, second, it is an expression of the unyielding family pride of the Curries. The other important image suggested with reference to Hagar Shipley is that of Hagar in the Old Testament (see IMAGES AND SYMBOLS). The name Hagar has, semantically, a root connected with the idea of fleeing. The Old Testament Hagar was a woman who twice had to flee from the house of Abraham and make her home in the wilderness. Hagar Shipley also tried to flee from her experiences. On one occasion, she left her husband to seek a new life on the coast. On the second occasion, she fled from Marvin and Doris to Shadow Point. Both experiences might be interpreted as representing flights into the wilderness, for the real answers to her problems lay in Manawaka and the memories of Manawaka. Fortunately, like the first Hagar, Hagar Shipley did receive her theophany: the Shadow Point experience was the beginning of the process which resulted in her judgement of herself.

Thus, the main burden of the novel is the change which comes to Hagar as a person. Her hardness melts and her egocentrism softens, in this way establishing a redemptive pattern for the novel (see STRUCTURE).

Finally, it is worth observing that the portrait of Hagar Shipley in *The Stone Angel* is not totally negative. She is not completely the Hecate-Crone of whom Margaret Atwood writes. The response which she evokes from us is not simply that of condemnation; we also feel for her both admiration and pathos. It is probably Hagar's valour which is the chief source of our admiration. She may be wrong --- indeed, she is often wrong --- but she is a doughty advocate. The little girl who stubbornly refused to cry when punished by her father became the courageous --- even if misguided --- woman who faced her isolation valiantly after her marriage. Her reflections concerning Matt's gift to her the night before her wedding reveal the strength and courage in her character:

> ... I wanted to go and talk with Matt, but I was not sure enough. He'd intended to send it as a reproach, a mockery, then found he cared something about me after all - that was my first thought. Then it struck me - what if he'd actually meant the gift to convey some gentleness, but changed his mind? If that was the case, I'd not have walked across the road to speak with him. I decided to

wait and see if he'd turn up the following day, to give me away in
place of Father. But, of course, he did not.   (p. 50)

With the same spirit, she began immediately to face the reality of the
life she had created in her marriage:

> The next day I got to work and scrubbed the house out. I
> planned to get a hired girl in the fall, when we had the cash. But in
> the meantime I had no intention of living in squalor. I had never
> scrubbed a floor in my life, but I worked that day as though I'd
> been driven by a whip.   (p. 52)

Nor was she lacking in physical courage. Assailed by the weakness of
her body in old age, nagged constantly by the searing pain under her
ribs, she fought her infirmities valiantly. Though exhausted and pain-
wracked, she struggled through the journey to Shadow Point, with only
the strength of her will to carry her on and enable her to endure. Even
at the end, close to death and humbled, her indomitable spirit asserted
itself in the simple act of seizing the glass of water from Doris:

> I only defeat myself by not accepting her. I know this - I know it
> very well. But I can't help it - it's my nature. I'll drink from this
> glass, or spill it, just as I choose. I'll not countenance anyone else's
> holding it for me. And yet - if she were in my place, I'd think her
> daft, and push her hands away, certain I could hold it for her
> better.
> I wrest from her the glass, full of water to be had for the taking.
> I hold it in my own hands. There. There.   (p. 308)

Here is Hagar in all the harshness of her self-reliance, but it is a picture
softened by admiration for her tenacity and for the vigour of her self-
assertiveness. In the final analysis, there is a sense of pathos in our
attitude towards her. She is still, after all, at the age of ninety like the
young Hagar who could respond to the sensuous sights and sounds
around her, capable of dreaming her romantic dreams, but incapable
of expressing the passions she feels. She is still at the age of ninety, in
spite of a "puffed face purpled with veins as though someone had
scribbled over the skin with an indelible pencil", the young woman
proud of her handsomeness. She is, above all, a human being who has
experienced the full weight of the tragic brevity of human life, which is
expressed so movingly by Mrs. Steiner:

> "Do you get used to life?" she says. "Can you answer me that?
> It all comes as a surprise. You get your first period, and you're
> amazed - *I can have babies now - such a thing!* When the children
> come, you think - *Is it mine? Did it come out of me? Who could
> believe it?* When you can't have them anymore, what a shock - *It's
> finished - so soon?"*
> I peer at her, thinking how peculiar that she knows so much.
>   (p. 104)

40

MRS. CURRIE

Mrs. Currie died in giving birth to Hagar, and so does not appear in the novel as a character.

The expensive stone angel which her husband bought to mark her burial place would seem to have been a rather ironic tribute to her, because she seems to have been quite unlike her proud, assertive husband. Hagar speaks of her mother's "feeble" ghost being relinquished in favour of her own "stubborn" one. The difference between Hagar and her mother is emphasized in the episode in which Hagar finds herself unable to play the part of her dead mother, in order to comfort Dan in his last hours of life (pp. 25ff). The character of Mrs. Currie is perhaps best summed up by her portrait, as described by Hagar:

> ... a spindly and anxious girl, rather plain, ringleted stiffly. She looks so worried that she will not know what to do, although she came of good family and ought not to have had a moment's hesitation about the propriety of her ways. But still she peers perplexed out of her little frame, wondering how on earth to please. (p. 59)

MARVIN SHIPLEY

Marvin was the first-born son of Bram and Hagar. When she went to hospital to bear her baby, Hagar felt deeply ashamed of her husband. She thought that she "wouldn't care to walk in broad daylight on the streets of Manawaka with any child of his" (p. 100). This response did not augur well for the child.

Indeed, as a child, Marvin received little warmth or affection from his mother. Work filled her time at this period, for she was determined that no one would ever be able to say that she did not keep a clean house. Consequently, Marvin received little attention from her. When he had finished his small chores, he would stand in the kitchen, waiting for words of approval from her. He did not receive them. To Hagar, Marvin was just 'getting on her nerves' and 'getting under her feet' (p. 112). Consequently, Marvin was more frequently in the company of his father, who gradually came to rely on his son for much of the work around the farm.

It is hardly surprising, in view of his home situation, that at the age of seventeen Marvin enlisted for service in the First War. The reaction of his parents to this action was predictable. Bram declared that Marvin would be well away from home. Hagar did nothing to prevent his enlistment, because "there was, after all, such a thing as duty, and Henry Pearl's eldest son had gone, and Jess's Vernon, and Gladys had two boys in the Army" (p. 129). When it came time for him to go, Marvin again sought to express and to receive some tenderness from his mother. On her part, Hagar wanted to "hold him tightly, plead with him, against all reason and reality, not to go", but she said nothing of her feelings; she did not want to "embarrass both of us, nor have him think I'd taken leave of my senses".

Marvin fought in the fierce battle of Vimy Ridge and survived the war. He did not return to Manawaka. After the war, he moved out to the coast and worked as a logger and longshoreman. Eventually, he went to work for Britemore Paint. Some years later he married Doris, and they had two children, Steven, who was an architect, and Tina. At the opening of the novel, Marvin and Doris had lived in Hagar's house for seventeen years.

According to Hagar, Marvin lacked the ability to be a conversationalist, and he wrote letters with poor spelling. These negative judgements are typical of Hagar. In fact, he had much to admire. He certainly had the tenacity and perseverance that John lacked: he had fought in the war, earned a satisfactory living for himself, and fathered two children who seemed to be successful. Neither was he lacking in sensitivity. When his father was dying, Marvin murmured that he was sorry, apparently voicing regret for the sterile relationships that had been a feature of the Shipley household, and for leaving his father to himself in that household. Moreover, he was manifestly unwilling to send his mother to Silverthreads, in spite of her ebullience and her physical infirmities. He is thus a rather wistful figure in the novel. At the age of sixty-four, he has a stomach ulcer, and yearns for peace and quiet. He still arouses his mother's contempt. However, he does at last win the recognition he deserves, when Hagar sees him as truly a faithful Jacob.

DORIS SHIPLEY

Like Marvin, Doris is the object of Hagar's scorn and contempt. According to Hagar, Doris resembles most "a broody hen", because of her "dowdy brown, dandruffed on either shoulder and down the back like molting feathers" (p. 29). Similarly, Hagar cannot stand what she describes as Doris's "mouse mask", and dismisses her daughter-in-law as a weak creature. Thus, even in the last moments of her life, Hagar is harsh with Doris, berating her slowness of action and comparing her apparent indecisiveness with her own assertiveness (p. 308).

Yet this is surely an unfair picture of Doris. She seems to be solicitous towards Hagar, making pots of tea for her mother-in-law, cooking meals that even Hagar judges to be good, taking her to the doctor, inviting her to church, looking after her bed linen. At her age, she is naturally tired, as even Hagar acknowledges at times, and her care of the irascible, rather paranoid Hagar must have taken a heavy toll of her strength. It is true that Doris is the prime mover in the plan to have Hagar enter Silverthreads, but her wish is understandable in view of the difficult circumstances which faced her.

AUNTIE DOLL STONEHOUSE

Auntie Doll was a widow who had kept house for Mr. Currie after the death of his wife. According to Hagar, she had thoughts that he might marry her, but her plain appearance and her lowly position negated any such possibility:

> ... it seemed a pity that she believed that Father held back because she was such a homely woman with her sallow skin that was never greatly improved by the witch hazel and lemon juice she dabbed on, and her incisors that protruded like a jack rabbit's. She was so conscious of those teeth of hers, she used to put one hand in front of her mouth when speaking, so that half the time even her words were hidden by a screen of fingers. But her appearance wasn't what would have decided Father. Matt and Dan and I always knew he could never have brought himself to marry his housekeeper.
>
> (p. 17)

It is one of the many touches of irony in the novel that Hagar, in spite of her condescension towards Auntie Doll, became herself a housekeeper, at Mr. Oatley's.

JASON CURRIE

There can be little doubt that the excessive pride which was Hagar's curse was an inheritance from her father. Pride and vanity seem to have been his outstanding characteristics. It was apparently pride, rather than grief or gratitude, which led to his erecting the stone angel in the Manawaka cemetery, and his final act, in providing for a memorial park in Manawaka, would seem justly to have been an act expressing his social vanity.

There is little hint that he was a man of much sensitivity. For example, he would seem to have had genuine affection for Lottie Drieser's mother, and yet after her death he made three significant comments:

> "Poor lass," he said. "She couldn't have had much of a life."
> Then, as though recalling himself, and to whom he spoke, "Her

sort isn't much loss to the town, I'm bound to say."
    Then an inexplicably startled look came over his face. "Consumption? That's contagious, isn't it? Well, the Lord works in wondrous ways His will to perform."
    None of the three made much sense to me then, but they stuck in my mind. I've since pondered - which was my father?   (p. 19)

In a sense, all three statements are a reflection of Mr. Currie. The first shows some feeling, though it is quickly swallowed up by the second, which is the utterance of the righteous Mr. Currie, a leading citizen of Manawaka. The third may well be the essential Mr. Currie who, having had some association with the unfortunate dead woman, was worried about the fact that she had died of a contagious disease. There is much justification for this view of him as an insensitive, unfeeling person. For example, Hagar's description of his grief after his wife's death contains more than simply a suggestion of spurious, hypocritical sorrow:

    ... When he said "your poor mother", the moisture would squeeze out from the shaggy eyelid, and I marveled that he could achieve it at will, so suitable and infinitely touching to the matrons of the town, who found a tear for the female dead a reassuring tribute to thankless motherhood.   (p. 59)

Moreover, his treatment of his own children displayed a grossly insensitive harshness. He had little patience with Daniel, who was delicate. He ignored Matt's pathetic attempts to provide for a brighter future by saving all the coins he could get. When Hagar announced her intention of marrying Bram Shipley, his main objection seemed to be that she had no right to make such a decision on her own. Once the marriage had taken place, he ignored his daughter, and when he died she received none of the considerable sum of money which he left.

    The picture of him, "coldly eying the camera, daring it not to do him justice" (p. 69), was as typical of his religious life as it was of all aspects of his life. He was strict in his devotions, never missing a Sunday service or the saying of grace at meals. Yet he was inordinately proud of his gift to the new church in Manawaka, for he whispered to his daughter, "I and Luke McVitie must've given the most, as he called our names first" (p. 16).

    Though his pride had tragic consequences, it was probably understandable in the light of the life he had led. The son of Sir Daniel Currie, he had come penniless to the prairies. That he achieved considerable prosperity by his own efforts is a tribute to his tenacity and labour. Little wonder, then, that he dwelt on the past glories of his family (p. 15).

44

Lottie Drieser

Lottie, "light as an eggshell" and with pale, fine hair, was an illegitimate child. Since her father was unknown or unidentified, she was contemptuously described by the boys in Manawaka as "No-Name" Lottie Drieser.

Nevertheless, she seemed to possess an inner strength which did not express itself aggressively. For example, in the secret visit to the funeral parlour, she was the only one of the children who dared to touch the dead face of Henry Pearl's baby sister. Moreover, when the children discovered distressed newly-hatched chicks on the town garbage dump, Lottie was the only child with the courage to kill them and so terminate their misery.

Because of her origins, Lottie was not welcomed socially by the respectable citizens of Manawaka. Mr. Currie was furious when he discovered that Dan had sneaked Lottie into a teenage party at the house. Yet, ironically, she fared better in life than Hagar. She married Telford Simmons, who eventually became mayor of Manawaka, and her prosperity made Hagar acutely aware of her own shabbiness. Futher, in order to finance her flight from the town with John, Hagar was obliged to sell some of her family possessions to Lottie.

Lottie was capable of exchanging sarcastic quips with Hagar, but on the whole she appears in the novel as a rather tragic person. An outcast as a child, she suffered the grief of the death of her only child, Arlene, in the senseless accident involving John. Her greatest grief --- again, ironically --- was caused by her alliance with Hagar, in an effort to frustrate the love between John and Arlene.

Daniel Currie

Dan, like his brother Matt, was "graceful" and "unspirited" and tried to please his father, but rarely succeeded in doing so. Unlike Matt, however, he "wouldn't lift a finger to work, unless he was pushed to it" (p. 21). Physically, he seems to have been a delicate boy, but Hagar observed --- typically --- that "he knew very well the advantages of poor health." This judgement would appear to be characteristic of the impatience both Mr. Currie and Hagar felt for Dan's weakness:

> ... Father had small patience with these antics, and used to say all
> Dan needed was fresh air and exercise. Sometimes he'd make Dan
> get up and get dressed, and would send him down to the store to
> clean out the warehouse. But sure as guns, if he did, the next day
> Dan would sprout chicken pox or something indisputable. It must
> have been mind over matter, for he cultivated illness as some
> people cultivate rare plants. Or so I thought then.   (pp. 21-22)

That Dan was genuinely delicate in health is evident from his death at the age of eighteen. The Currie children had been skating on the Wachakwa river when Dan fell through the ice. As a result, he developed pneumonia, from which he died. In the last hours of his life, Dan needed his mother, "the woman," Hagar observed, "Dan was said to resemble so much and from whom he'd inherited a frailty I could not help but detest" (p. 25). Matt wanted Hagar to wear their mother's shawl and comfort Dan. However, Hagar could not bring herself to play the part of "that meek woman", and it was left to Matt to play out the role.

When Daniel was well, he was happy and carefree, "like a water beetle busily boating on the surface of life" (p. 22). The measure of the difference between his personality and that of his father can be gauged from the fact that he sneaked the unwanted Lottie into one of their teenage parties.

MATT CURRIE

Matt was similar to his brother Dan, in that they both took after their mother, and not their father, whom Hagar resembled most. Unlike Dan, Matt was not frail physically, though he was "skinny and bespectacled". However, his clumsiness enraged his father when he worked in the store.

Matt was a creature of dreams who received no sympathy or encouragement from his father. When he was sixteen, he asked his father for a rifle, so that he could set traplines at Galloping Mountain. His father refused, grumbling at the possible expense if Matt were to get hurt. As a child, Matt used to save his pennies feverishly. In later years, Hagar learned from Auntie Doll that Matt's purpose was to get money to set up in business for himself or to study law down East. When he was almost seventeen, however, "it finally dawned on him that the handful of nickels and quarters he had wouldn't take him far" (p. 21). Consequently, he spent all of his money buying a fighting cock, which had to be killed after its first, unsuccessful battle. Another dream had been shattered. A third blow for Matt came when Hagar was sent away to school. Even Hagar, knowing how much it meant to him, thought that he should have been the one to go, but Mr. Currie would suffer no argument over his decision. It was too late, he declared, for Matt, who was past twenty, to go to school. Anyway, Mr. Currie continued, he was needed at the store, and he could "learn all he needs right here, if he's minded to do so" (p. 42). Thus Hagar said nothing of her feelings to Matt.

The effect of his home life upon Matt can be discerned from

his marriage. He married Mavis, and they loved one another. However, they did not have children. The absence of children was clearly a deliberate choice. Knowing the unhappiness he had experienced, Matt did not want children of his own. It was to be expected, then, that when faced by death during an influenza epidemic, Matt surrendered his life without a struggle, as Auntie Doll makes clear:

> "He went quietly," she said. He didn't fight his death, as some do. They only make it harder for themselves. Matt seemed to know there was no help for it, Mavis said. He didn't struggle to breathe, or try to hang on. He let himself slip away." (p. 60)

MR. TROY

Mr. Troy, the minister of the church attended by Doris and Marvin, is described contemptuously by Hagar as "God's little man" (p. 40). He visited Hagar at the request of Doris, partly to put the old woman in a frame of mind for accepting Silver Threads, but he was no match for Hagar. She enjoyed watching him flounder when trying to say the right thing to her, and dismissed his words scornfully:

> ... He speaks of prayer and comfort, all in a breath, as though God were a kind of feather bed or spring-filled mattress. I nod and nod and nod. Easier to agree, now, hoping he will soon go. He prays a little prayer, and I bow my head, a feather in his cap or in the eiderdown of God. Then, mercifully, he leaves. (p. 53)

Yet, ironically, Mr. Troy proved to be the vital force in effecting the change which came to Hagar. He visited her in hospital towards the end of her life. She still had a little patience with him (p. 291). However, when he sang a hymn for her, Hagar's attitude began to change. She admired his courage in complying with her request, and she was astonished at the firmness and sureness of his singing. The hymn wrought its effect. Hagar was reduced to tears, in a moment of regret that came with shattering bitterness. Mr. Troy felt that he had failed again, but Hagar knew that he had not, though she was charact-eristically unable to reassure him. Nevertheless, he had been the unwitting and ironic instrument of her redemption.

BRAM SHIPLEY

Bram Shipley was spurned by the respectable citizens of Man-awaka. Mr. Currie described him as being "as common as dirt", and thus echoed the phrase that even Lottie used. Certainly, he could not be described as a successful man. He was thirty-eight when Hagar met him at the dance, and had been married previously. He had come from the East with his wife Clara some years before, and had a farm just outside the town. The farm was on river land and should have been good, but it was not.

Hagar had seen him in the store on a number of occasions, and she recalled that he laughed constantly. The source of his laughter was a puzzle, for his wife had died, leaving him alone to raise two daughters.

Compared with Hagar, he was a rough, uncouth person. Yet strangely, these very qualities attracted Hagar to him, as her account of their dancing makes evident:

> We spun around the chalky floor, and I reveled in his finger-nails with crescents of ingrown earth that never met a file. I fancied I heard in his laughter the bravery of battalions. I thought he looked a bearded Indian, so brown and beaked a face. The black hair thrusting from his chin was rough as thistles. The next instant, though, I imagined him rigged out in a suit of gray soft as a dove's breast-feathers. (p. 45)

Evidently, something in him awakened the sensuality within Hagar. For example, later, when he outraged her by pressing his groin against her, she still accepted when he asked her to dance again. After their marriage, Hagar found herself responding to his flesh, so that she felt her "blood and vitals" rise to meet his. Her later judgement of their relationship was thus true: "His banner over me was his skin."

Hagar never spoke of her response to Bram, and he never noticed it. He did not notice it because he "had an innocence about him". This observation of Hagar's contains a great deal of truth. Though shabby and unkempt in appearance, and though rough in speech and action, there seemed to be a strange tenderness within Bram. He seemed to love Hagar genuinely when they were married, though she did not recognize it as love (p. 80). After their wedding, he offered her a gift which was obviously a gift of love, but she treated it with characteristic indifference:

> ... When we entered, Bram handed me a cut-glass decanter with a silver top.
> "This here's for you, Hagar."
> I took it so casually, and laid it aside, and thought no more about it. He picked it up in his hands and turned it around. For a moment I thought he meant to break it, and for the life of me I couldn't see why. Then he laughed and set it down and came close to me.
> "Let's see what you look like under all that rig-out, Hagar."
> (p. 51)

This no doubt set the tone of their relationship. Bram seemed to offer love in his own unsophisticated way, but Hagar rebuffed the offering by her silence. He knew nothing of her real response to him, being offered only her icy scorn. Her feelings remained unspoken throughout their marriage. Hagar was silent when her flesh responded to him; she was silent when he was so deeply affected by the loss of his favourite horse; and she was silent when he faced death.

Hagar's treatment of him provoked Bram into · greater excesses of surly, irresponsible behaviour. He deliberately wore his roughness as a garment of pride. Thus, when Charlotte Tappen teased him by speaking enthusiastically of the Glee Club's forthcoming performance of *The Messiah,* he declared defiantly that he did not "give a good goddam" (p. 70). In church, he mortified Hagar by whispering critical remarks about the minister. He drank defiantly with his crony, Charlie Bean, spending nights in the barn when he knew that his drunken presence would be unwelcome in the house. As a result, the marriage was a trap for both of them: "Twenty-four years, in all, were scoured away like sandbanks under the spate of our wrangles and bicker" (p. 116). Bram and Hagar had married one another under the delusion that each could change the behaviour of the other. The dream foundered on the rock of Hagar's pride.

The relationship was tragic. Bram could have been a different man. He was not lazy. He could work "like fury and would come in at supper time smelling of sweat and sun" (p. 113), but his values were different from those of his wife. Hagar's values were founded on the social approval of others. She wanted Bram to do well, "so that people in Manawaka, whether they liked him or not, would at least be forced to respect him" (p. 84). But Bram marched to a different drummer. He could work hard when he wanted to, but then "he would recall the brown Wachakwa, the easeful grass on the sloping banks, and he'd be off, like Simple Simon, to fish for whales, maybe, in six inches of creek water" (p. 113). Prosperity was not a force that motivated him. Thus, when the farm was growing wheat successfully, Bram wanted to switch to breeding saddle horses, because he was "crazy about horses." His point of view was typical: "Let somebody else cash in ... I got enough to buy what I want" (p. 83).

In the end, Bram's drinking caused his death, through the deterioration of his liver. In his last days, the broadness of his shoulders vanished, and his mind wandered. But only Marvin expressed to his uncomprehending father his sorrow for the past. To the end, Hagar was silent:

> ... I went to his room, but he was only talking in his sleep. He lay

curled up and fragile in the big bed where we'd coupled and it made me sick to think I'd lain with him, for now he looked like an ancient child. Looking down at him, a part of me could never stand him, what he's been, and yet that moment I'd willingly have called him back from where he'd gone to say even once what Marvin had said, and with as much bewilderment, not knowing who to fault for the way the years had turned ... But there was nothing I could do for him, nothing he needed now, so I went back to Marvin's old room where I slept.   (p. 183)

In one of the many ironies of the novel, Bram's reputation enjoyed rehabilitation of a kind. When Hagar visited the Manawaka cemetery years later, a young caretaker pointed out the gravestone which bore both the name Currie and the name Shipley. They were, he explained, two of the earliest pioneering families in the district, and had been connected by marriage. His words marked the end of the past. The years had extinguished the angry fires of conflict and the power of the seemingly important values and pride that both Hagar and her father had cherished. The differences marked by Bram's rebellious act of urinating on the steps of Mr. Currie's store had disappeared. The two families were one: "Both the same. Nothing to pick and choose between them now. That was as it should be" (p.306).

JOHN SHIPLEY

John was the second-born son of Bram and Hagar. Hagar found his birth an easy one - "not more than six hours' labour" (p. 122) - and the ease of his birth was perhaps symbolic of his difference from Marvin. Unlike Marvin, he was a slight child, who moved quickly: "He ran everywhere, a walking pace being too slow for him" (p. 123).

Hagar quickly regarded her new son as a Currie rather than as a Shipley:

"A pity," I used to say to him. "A great pity your grandfather never saw you, for you're a boy after his own heart. Never mind. You may not have his money, but you've got his get-up-and-go."
(p. 123)

Thus, she used to tell him about the past glories of the Currie family, and it was to John that she gave the Currie plaid-pin. She also tried to educate John a little more earnestly than she did Marvin.

Unfortunately, Hagar saw in John only what she wanted to see. She tended to ignore, or excuse, the early signs of his wildness:

... He was as wild as mustard seed in some ways, that child. He'd

50

> come out with swear words that would curl your hair, and I knew
> where he'd got them. After he started school, the teacher some-
> times sent me a note (through the mail, not trusting John to deliver
> it) saying he'd been caught fighting again, and I'd scold him all
> right but I don't know that it ever did much good.   (p. 127)

He also had a knack for "gathering the weirdest crew". Amongst his early friends were the Tonnere boys, French half-breeds whom Hagar scorned. It was with these boys that John played the game of walking over the narrow railway bridge that crossed the Wachakwa river. That game was, years later, to lead to John's death, when he drove a car across the bridge and met an unexpected freight train.

John's real character emerged during the years that he lived on the coast with Hagar. When they began their flight, he revealed that he had traded the Currie plaid-pin for a knife. That revelation was an omen of what was to come. John proved to be a deceitful person who possessed a superficial charm. He invented fictitious friends whom he said he had met at school, much to Hagar's embarrassment when she telephoned one of the parents (p. 157). He also lied to his girlfriends, claiming that Mr. Oatley was his uncle. Further, he had none of Marvin's steady application to work. Dreamily fitfully about a grandiose future, he was unable to keep a permanent job. Finally, he proved plainly his lack of desire to pursue the ambitions Hagar had for him, when he announced his intention of returning to Manawaka and the Shipley farm.

He proved his identification with Bram on his return to the prairies. He dressed in Bram's old clothes, cursed the way Bram did, and drank as his father did. His behaviour was obviously a deliberate, calculated denial of all that his mother valued.

The one redeeming aspect of his life was his love for Arlene. Typical of John, their love began in a spirit of mockery and teasing, for he did not believe that Arlene would every marry a "Shitley" (p. 174). He became truly aware of the sincerity of Arlene's love when he learned that she had driven him home from a dance at which he had got drunk. That love ended in tragedy, for Hagar and Lottie conspired to prevent it, by having Arlene go down East for a year. One evening, drunk for the first time in months, John accepted a bet to drive his car across the railway bridge. The result was death for Arlene and for himself.

John had begun to change, as the cessation in his drinking demonstrated, but Hagar had not detected the change. She wanted John to be a person in her mould. She had judged wrongly, and her error had afflicted all of John's life. Ironically, John knew the truth that she could not recognize: " 'You always bet on the wrong horse,' John said gently. 'Marv was your boy, but you never saw that, did you?" (p. 237).

STRUCTURE

The structure of *The Stone Angel* has a deceptively easy tempo. Flowing smoothly in a kind of rhythmic counterpoint, its story unfolds with an artful naturalness. Events of the present, experienced by Hagar as she sits restlessly in her Vancouver home or muses confusedly by the shore at Shadow Point or lies impatiently in hospital awaiting death, summon up the recollection of past scenes with a smoothness that is both charming and convincing. On occasion, the recollections emerge briefly, creating a mood of nostalgia which contrast sharply with the unpleasantness reality of the present. Thus, for example, in chapter one, when Hagar mentions with vanity the dress she is wearing, a "lilac silk", which is "real silk, mine, spun by worms in China", she is contrasting her mode of dress with the "drab shades" of Doris, who "wouldn't know silk from flour sacks". And then her talk of the lilac silk triggers memories:

> The lilac is the exact same shade as the lilacs that used to grow beside the gray front porch of the Shipley place. There was little enough time or room for flowering shrubs there, with that land that was never lucky from the first breaking of the ground, all the broken machinery standing in the yard like the old bones and ribs of great dead sea creatures washed to shore, and the yard muddy and puddled with yellow ammonia pools where the horses emptied themselves. The lilacs grew with no care given them, and in the early summer they hung like bunches of mild mauve grapes from branches with leaves like dark green hearts, and the scent of them was so bold and sweet you could smell nothing else, a seasonal mercy. (p. 29)

The memory vanishes in a moment. Its place is taken swiftly by the presence of Doris, "fatly smirking." But it has wrought its effect. Full of sweetness, suggestive of the hidden sensuality of Hagar's nature, it has, by its mood magic, helped to establish the flow of the narrative. The breeze of the past has wafted into the present, bringing with it nostalgic colour and warmth. At other times, something in the present prompts a more extended recollection, and an entire scene is revealed. This occurs, for example, in chapter two, where the technique for this weaving together of past and present is interesting to observe. On that occasion, Hagar is casting her eyes over her collection of photographs. The pictures of her mother and her father evoke memories of their contrasting natures, and then the recollection of her own birth, which was at the expense of her mother's death. For a moment, Hagar's gaze moves to the gilt-edged mirror which used to hang in the downstairs hall of the Currie house. This causes her to remember the way in which she would glance in the mirror when she passed it, wondering why her brothers had inherited their mother's daintiness, while she was "bit-boned and husky as an ox." This memory turns her attention to the picture of herself at twenty. She reflects that while she was not pretty, she was handsome. In turn, this thought of her own solid hand-someness brings to mind the contrast offered by "delicate-seeming women", and in particular by Matt's wife, Mavis, "whose health had always been precarious." From that point on, the story turns to events in Manawaka, beginning with Matt's death (p. 60) and ending with Mr. Currie's death (pp. 63-64). The progression is accomplished without awkwardness or artificiality. Thoughts of the photographs have led Hagar's eyes to the mirror and on to the picture of herself at twenty. Reflections on her own appearance have then led naturally to Mavis.

The first aspect of the structure, then, is its tempo, which is characterized --- in metaphorical terms --- as fluid, a kind of natural flow which lends to Hagar's recollections an air of spontaneity and a tone of credibility. The techniques for achieving this effect are interesting to observe, and the following examples of the weaving of past and present are worth further study:

---- the transition from "Silverthreads" to the birth of Marvin (p.99).

---- the change from the conversation with Mr. Troy to the account of Marvin's birth (p. 121).

---- the different technique by which the transition from the past to the present is achieved (p. 136)

---- the theme of "waiting" which accomplishes the link between past and present when Hagar is at Shadow Point (p. 160)

The techniques are demanded, of course, by the very nature of the plot of the novel. *The Stone Angel* is, in a sense, two stories woven together and finding their unity in the central character, Hagar Shipley. One story concerns Hagar at the age of ninety, cumbersomely fat and racked by physical illness, seeking to avoid the threat of Silverthreads, the home to which Marvin and Doris wish her to go. Her grumbling discontent with her situation and her fearful suspicion of her son and daughter-in-law permeate this part of the narrative. This aspect of the plot moves to a moving and intriguing crisis with her retreat to Shadow Point and the encounter with Murray Lees. From that point on, the story proceeds fairly quickly towards its resolution with the death of Hagar in the hospital. That is one aspect of the dual plot. The other deals with past events which portray Hagar in the years

54

of her youth, middle age and that part of the period of old age which precedes her situation as the novel opens. On the one hand, that story helps to make clear the context of living which has led to Hagar's situation and personality. Her character emerges from her responses to the past in the past, and from her responses to the past at the time experiences are being recollected. Her present predicament --- and her attitude towards it --- becomes explicit and comprehensible in the light of the recollections. On the other hand, the recollections of the past have an important effect on present thoughts and actions. The uncovering of the past by Hagar leads to the uncovering of feelings, attitudes, values and judgements which had not been fully appreciated and explored at an earlier time. As a result of this uncovering, Hagar comes to a new understanding of her own life and character. This is a process whose critical stage is the encounter with Murray Lees, and which leads inexorably to Hagar's last conversation with Marvin, to whom she lies in a spirit of compassion that has hitherto been quite alien to her nature. Thus, clearly, there are in a sense two plots which eventually converge. The Hagar of the past emerges to confront the Hagar of the present. From the confrontation, there springs a new Hagar, still the doughty, indomitable fighter, still ruggedly and fear-somely independent in spirit, but a new Hagar whose has laid to rest the ghosts of the past. Her stubbornness, her pride, her egotism, her harshness, - all have been laid bare and recognized for what they are. Therefore, at the end Hagar is able to undertake her act of redemption in her compassionate words to Marvin, who is at last granted the peace for which he had earnestly toiled.

This duality in the plot leads to another pattern which is char-acteristic of the structure of the novel, and that is the pattern suggested by a major theme - the redemption of Hagar Shipley. As the novel opens, she is an unregenerate old woman, stubborn and irascible, who has not faced her age with a sense of peace. As the story unfolds, the source of her discontent gradually emerges. It lies somewhere in the buried past which the novel uncovers little by little. Though that uncov-ering is gradual, it is nonetheless persistent and irresistible. It is something which *has* to be done. Hagar is "caught up" (p. 6) in the process of remembering. Marvin and Doris may misunderstand what is happening; they may simply say, "Mother's having one of her days". Hagar herself may resist the activity, vowing that she will not remember her "lost men". But remember she must, for buried in those memories lies whatever she needs to cope adequately with the present situation. As a result, the story assumes a certain pattern which Clara Thomas described as "sacramental". Thus, elements of the Christian pattern of the progression from sin to salvation can be discerned. In the beginning, through the picture of Hagar in her earlier years and Hagar at the age of ninety, the unrepentant sinner looms large. Restrained and self-contained, Hagar has lived for herself. Proud of her own strength, she was unable, for example, to act the part of her weaker mother by wearing her mother's shawl, when Daniel lay dying. Headstrong and stubborn, she married Bram Shipley against all the urgings of her father and all the dictates of common sense. Doggedly, she refused her husband any sign of love, even when her flesh responded to his with warmth and affection. Coldly, she spurned Marvin as a child, seeing in him only the image of the uncouth Bram. Cynically, she manipulated John's life, trying desperately to mould it as she would have it. And at last in old age, she contemptuously accepted the ministrations of Marvin and Doris. In this way, she wrought havoc in the lives of those around her. She appears, then, in a major part of the novel very much as the unrepentant sinner. Yet, from that, the novel progresses towards its resolution in the redemptive pattern. Hagar is not satisfied with what her life has been. The escape to Shadow Point becomes symbolic of an attempt to get rid of the burden of the past. As though returning to the gray Shipley place, she takes up residence in the unpainted cannery house, and her response shows her to be ready for change: "To move to a new place - that's the greatest excitement. For a while you believe you carry nothing with you - all is cancelled from before, or cauterized, and you begin again and nothing will go wrong again." (p.155) However, the past remains; it must still be dealt with. Nevertheless, Hagar is obviously not satisfied with it:

> And here am I, the same Hagar, in a different establishment once more, and waiting again. I try, a little, to pray, as one's meant to do at evening, thinking perhaps the knack of it will come to me here. But it works no better than it ever did. I can't change what's happened to me in my life, or make what's not occurred take place. But I can't say I like it, or accept it, or believe it's for the best. I don't and never shall, not even if I'm damned for it.
>
> (p. 160)

Thus, like the Ancient Mariner of Coleridge's poem, Hagar is parched with thirst. The thirst is, of course, symbolic of the thirst for peace, for forgiveness, for salvation. Like the Ancient Mariner, she has, she feels, some albatross to atone for (p. 186). At this moment, her spirit is ripe for new life. Symbolically, she finds a new kind of union with nature. She drinks from the water bucket from which the "raucous gang" of sparrows has drunk, and though the water is "murky and tastes of soil and fallen leaves and rust", she cannot find it in herself to complain (p. 187). Afterwards, she walks to the sea, and her observations of the peace and gentleness of the scene show a heightened sense of perception:

... The air is salted, sturdy with the scent of fish. The shore is cobbled with white sea-washed stones that clatter and slide under my unsure feet. Great logs, broken away from booms and drifted ashore, lie along the beach like natural benches. The sea is green and clear. In the shallows I can see to the bottom, down where the stones which are actually dun and dull olive and slate have been changed underwater and shimmer wetly as though they were garnets and opals and slabs of jade. A dark bulb of kelp floats languidly like a mermaid, trailing its strands and frilled leaves of brownish yellow hair. A few cast-off clam shells, gutted by gulls, perhaps, just from the watery sand like discarded saucers in a sea midden. A crab walks delicately on its pincered claws.   (p. 187)

Ripe for change, Hagar is visited by Murray Lees. In the warmth of the companionship of this man, who has also suffered the loss of a son, she tells of the circumstances of John's death. The story has a cathartic effect upon her. It is an act of repentance following a confession of sin, though even then Hagar refers to it "as though it were worms, to be purged" (p. 245). When she awakes from the sleep which follows her story, the full effect of her confession is clear. In contrast with her previous abrasive strength, she feels a new timidity (p. 247). Confusing Lees with her dead son John, she receives the forgiveness which the sinner craves:

I'm feeling better now. I'm resting easy. My hand remains on his wrist. So thin it is that I can feel the fine bones through the skin and the quick beating of his pulse. If there's a time to speak, it's surely now.

'I didn't really mean it, about not bringing her here. A person speaks in haste. I've always had a temper. I wouldn't want you to feel you always had to be going out somewhere. You could come here in the evenings. I wouldn't say a word. I could go into the front room, or upstairs, if you liked. I'd not get in your way. Wouldn't that be a good idea?'

I've spoken so calmly, so reasonably. He can't in all conscience refuse what I've said. I wait. At last I hear his voice. An inexplicable sound, a grating, like a groan or a sob. I grow anxious, and think he may still be angry. But when he speaks, his voice is not angry at all.

'It's okay,' he says. 'I knew all the time you never meant it. Everything is all right. You try to sleep. Everything's quite okay.'

I sigh, content. He pulls the blanket up around me. I could even beg God's pardon this moment, for thinking ill of Him some time or other.   (pp. 247-248)

The forgiveness is complete. Thus, when Lees leaves after the arrival of

Marvin and Doris, Hagar is sorry to see him go, for she felt that it was "a kind of mercy" that she had encountered him. The significance of this moment becomes completely clear to Hagar only later, however. It happens during Mr. Troy's visit to the hospital. It is then that the full act of contrition is undertaken, and the conscious confession made (p. 292). As a result, a new gentleness comes to Hagar. She speaks gently to Doris, assuring her that Mr. Troy's visit was beneficial, though Doris does not believe what is said (p. 293). Later, she has a new awareness of the burdens of others; she sees that her grandson, Steven, is "troubled by things I know nothing of" (p. 297). However, her new awareness and her new compassion emerge most vividly and movingly in her final conversation with Marvin. She sees him in a new light; he, not John, is "truly Jacob". To him at the last she must give her blessing: "And I see I am thus strangely cast, and perhaps have been so from the beginning, and can only release myself by releasing him" (p. 304). Consequently, though tempted to ask her son's pardon, she resists her impulse; she must not receive blessing but give blessing. Thus she tells Marvin that he has been a good son, "A better son than John." Hagar's redemption is complete, and this prepares the reader for the final moment in the novel, as Hagar drinks symbolically from the water-glass. Drinking as though from the cup of salvation, taking the water of life, she knows peace (p. 308).

It is clear that a pattern of redemption emerges to give shape to the narrative. The pattern is not, of course, rigid, because no exact allegory of the path of Christian salvation can be intended. The novel is not a Christian homily. However, the lines of progression are clear as they move towards Hagar's final moments, and may be summarized in the following way:

Hagar the unregenerate: this section would include all of the events from Hagar's past and the events preceding her flight to Shadow Point. In these experiences, she is frequently unable to speak of her real emotions and unable to express tenderness. Her fierce pride blights the lives of others.

Hagar confronting herself: alone at Shadow Point, she awakens to nature and feels impending judgement.

Hagar's act of contrition: confusing Lees with John, she speaks the words of reconciliation which she had previously been unable to utter.

Hagar's confession: deeply moved by the hymn which Mr. Troy sings, she confesses her sin to herself, aware at last of the chains which had bound her and which had "shackled" all whom she touched.

Hagar's forgiveness: freed by her new vision, Hagar is able to bring blessing to Marvin's life. In the very act of giving blessing, she receives the pardon for which she had not asked.

Hagar's redemption: though losing none of her fierce independence, Hagar at last grasps the cup offered to her by Doris, who has insistently sought to bring to Hagar the comforts of religion.

Also discernible is a fourth structural pattern in *The Stone Angel*, and that is the use of parallel scenes and events. In structural terms, this technique most often supplies the link between past and present in the book. In addition, of course, these parallels add shades of meaning to both sides of the comparison. The parallels may be identified as follows:

1. The "escape" motif.

The significance of this *motif* can be found in Hagar's sojourn at Shadow Point. Rummaging in the old house beside the cannery, she find an old pair of brass scales without weights. As she observes them, she remarks, "Nothing can be weighed here and found wanting" (p. 154). The words possess symbolic meaning, of course. Hagar's entire act of recollecting the past has been an act of "weighing", of remembering in order to assess the significance of what has happened and to relate it to events in the present. Now, at Shadow Point, Hagar feels --- wrongly --- that the weighing process is over, that she has a new beginning, unburdened by the past. Thus, as she lies down to sleep, she is "heartened", and declares,

> To move to a new place - that's the greatest excitement. For a while you believe you carry nothing with you - all is cancelled from before, or cauterized, and you begin again and nothing will go wrong this time. (p. 155)

Hagar is wrong. The past cannot be left behind. It is not "cancelled." It must be encountered, and she must come to terms with it once and for all. This is what actually happens at Shadow Point, and it happens dramatically through the unhappy figure of Murray Lees. Through her strange communion with him, Hagar is finally able to say what she has been unable to say before. The tenderness within her is freed and expresses itself in what she believes to be a reconciliation with her dead son, John. The drama is full of ironies that underline the futility of Hagar's attempt to escape the past. It takes place in the midst of the old, unpainted cannery buildings, which are reminiscent of the gray Shipley place, and it is accomplished through the medium of a character whose drinking and language remind one of the uncouth behaviour of Bram. The past surrounds Hagar. Far from 'carrying nothing with her' to Shadow Point, she has carried the whole weight of the past with her and finally been able to uncover it for what it is.

Hagar's flight to Shadow Point was a futile attempt to escape. In this aspect, it is a reminder of an earlier attempt by Hagar to escape. That occurred when she took John from Manawaka and out to the coast, where she worked for Mr. Oatley. There, Hagar discovered that she could not escape her beginnings, nor the life she had left on the prairies. To begin with, the setting for her supposedly new life was somewhat unreal, as her description of Mr. Oatley and his residence reveals:

> That house of Mr. Oatley's - like a stone barn, it was, gigantic, and he there alone, living in his library, speaking feelingly of his love for the classics and slipping detective novels between the calf-bound covers of *Xenophon's Anabasis,* scarcely setting foot in the drawing-rooms and yet insisting that everything be kept up to scratch for the visitors who never came. (p. 155)

The setting is emphasized by the description of Mr. Oatley's exotic garden, with its lawns "like green ballrooms" and its unusual trees --- "wine-leaved plum, monkey trees with blackish green arms, skinny and simian" (p. 156). No less an important part of the setting were Mr. Oatley's exotic stories of his past:

> He'd been in shipping and said they used to bring Oriental wives here, when the celestials were forbidden to bring their women, and charge huge sums for passage, and pack the females like tinned shrimp in the lower hold, and if the Immigration men scented the hoax, the false bottom was levered open, and the women plummeted. They knew the chance they took when they began, he assured me. The husbands were always angry, both women and passage money lost, but who could help it? And Mr. Oatley would shrug and smile, begging my laughter and my approbation.
> (p. 156)

The stories sound as though belong more among Mr. Oatley's detective fiction than in reality. However, they do contribute to the emphasis upon Hagar's flight from Manawaka as a flight into fantasy. It was not, and could not be, a solution to the problems that life in Manawaka had revealed. Thus, life at Mr. Oatley's was "becalmed"; it was simply "a period of waiting and of marking time" (p. 160). It was John who brought the flight to an end. Through him, the full irony of Hagar's attempt to escape became clear. For John proved to be another Bram.

Attempting to escape Bram, she had brought Bram in miniature with
her. True, John had a charm that his father lacked; John could "charm
the birds off the trees when he wanted to" (p.156). But he was an
inveterate liar: he lied about the friends he had, and he lied about the
position Hagar occupied at Mr. Oatley's. Like his father, he had the
capacity for growing enthusiastic about dreams of the future (p. 158);
but, unlike Marvin, he did not possess the steadiness required to
provide himself with security. John was, in a sense, the embodiment of
Bram and Manawaka. Thus, when his mother tries to dissuade him
from returning home, his words have added significance:

> "You've forgotten what he's like," I said. "You'll not stay.
> You'll soon see, once you get there."
> "I haven't forgotten," John said.
> "Why go, then? There's nothing for you there."
> "You never know," he said. "I might get on famously. Maybe
> it's just the place for me."
> His laughter was incomprehensible to me.   (p. 167)

Of course John's laughter was incomprehensible to Hagar. He knew
what she did not: that he was truly Bram's son, not Hagar's. She had
sought to ensure that he would be all that she wanted by taking him
from his father, and she had failed. New beginnings were not made by
endeavouring to cancel out the past, in spite of Hagar's optimistic
words which stand as a motto at the beginning of the account of life at
Mr. Oatley's (p. 155).

2. "Playing house"

The concept of playing house occurs in two specific incidents
in the novel, both in chapter 7. On the first occasion, Hagar is watching
two children playing on the beach at Shadow Point. The boy is
searching for clam shells, which he offers to the little girl, remarking
that they can serve as bowls for their game. The girl, rather crisply and
domineeringly, contradicts the boy. They have enough bowls, she says;
the shells will be plates. Under her firm direction, everything is "tidy
and organized". However, when her companion tries to participate
again by pretending that their log is a cupboard, the girl again contradicts him: the log, she declares, is their table. Her domineering manner
prompts Hagar to make an observation: "Stupid girl. She knows
nothing. Why won't she praise him a little? She's so sharp with him.
He'll become fed up in a minute" (p. 188). But the girl does not become
gentler; she shrieks at the boy, calling him "a stupid bloody bum!" The
ensuing quarrel is more than Hagar can resist; she yields "to the
terrible temptation to straighten their situation" (p. 189). Hagar's
attempt fails, as the children run away in fear, and Hagar is left cursing
her own stupidity: "Oh, stupid, stupid - how could I have been so dull

in the wits? ... Why did I speak? I can never leave well enough alone"
(p. 189). This inability to "leave well enough alone" triggers Hagar's
memory. She recalls another occasion when she could not leave well
enough alone. She remembers "some other children, once, playing at
house, but in a somewhat different manner" (p. 192). The other
children she remembers are, of course, John and Arlene, and the
children playing on the beach were a miniature image of what had
happened long ago. John and Arlene had been truly in love, as Hagar
realized when she overheard them one day:

> Nothing to bless themselves with, they had, not a penny in the
> bank, a gray shell of a house around them, and outside a grit-filled
> wind that blew nobody any good, and yet they'd closed themselves
> to it all and opened only to each other. It seemed incredible that
> such a spate of unapologetic life should flourish in this mean and
> crabbed world.   (p. 208)

In their love, they played house. "Let's say this is our house," Arlene
had exclaimed (p. 207), and she and John had made love and,
afterwards, had a meal together in their "playhouse". Yet, in spite of
the obvious signs of their love, Hagar had not been able to leave well
alone. When the young couple left the house, she went up to bed,
"planning what to do" (p. 209). Her plans were directed towards
separating the young couple and had tragic consequences. Her actions
resulted in further rebelliousness from John and in the fatal automobile
accident that took his life and the life of Arlene. Not until her
encounter with Murray Lees was Hagar able to admit her folly; not
until that moment did she express her sorrow for what had happened.
Her reflections over her attitude to the children is the beginning of the
redemptive pattern for her. Thus, the parallelism in these two incidents
of "playing house" is important for the novel as a whole.

There is, perhaps, some very pointed irony in this structural
element in the novel, because, in a sense, Hagar herself could be
accused of having played house, instead of living in an open and honest
relationship. For example, when she first met Bram Shipley at the
school dance, she was playing a game, losing herself in fantasy:

> Oh, I was the one, all right, tossing my black mane contempt-
> uously, yet never certain the young men had really noticed. I knew
> my mind, no doubt, but the mind changed every minute, one
> instant feeling pleased with what I knew and who I was and where
> I lived, the next instant consigning the brick house to perdition
> and seeing the plain board town and the shack dwellings beyond
> our pale as though They'd been the beckoning illustrations in the
> book of Slavic fairy tales given me by an aunt, the enchanted
> houses with eyes, walking on their own splayed hen's feet, the
> czar's sons playing at peasants in coarse embroidered tunics,
> bloused and belted, the ashen girls drowning attractively in meres,

62

> crowned always with lilies, never with pigweed or slime.   (p. 46)

In such a mood, all of Bram's unattractive features were transformed in her sight. In his laughter she heard "the bravery of battalions", and to her he looked like "a bearded Indian" (p. 45). She undertakes to marry Bram with the same kind of irresponsible playfulness. She defies her father, "drunk with exhiliration" (p. 49) at her daring. She goes to Bram's home thinking of herself as "chatelaine" (p. 51). Reality proves to be very different from fantasy, as Hagar learns:

> And yet - here's the joker in the pack - we'd each married for those qualities we later found we couldn't bear, he for my manners and speech, I for his flouting of them.   (p. 79)

The result was a bond without affection, a relationship whose poison spread to the children of the marriage. Truly indeed, Hagar knew what it was to play at house, for she had done so herself.

From the foregoing, then, it would seem that there are four important structural elements in *The Stone Angel:*

1. **Tempo:** the movement from present to past and back to present events again gives to the novel a distinctive rhythm.

2. **Dual plot:** the novel is the weaving together of two plots. One is the story of the events which have shaped Hagar's life to the point at which the novel begins. The other Hagar's confrontation with the crises of her last days. After the retreat to Shadow Point, the two plots are more closely fused from a narrative point of view and are submerged in the major concern, which is the preparation of Hagar's spirit for death.

3. **The spiritual pattern:** as the novel unfolds, it becomes obvious that Hagar is not simply bent on fondly recalling memories. She is, indeed, "rampant with memory", but the act of recollection becomes more and more purposeful, until at last she is able to respond with a compassion that had been absent earlier in her life.

4. **Motif:** structural unity is achieved, in part, through the use of parallel incidents which take on the force and significance of *motifs.* Two of the important parallels have been discussed in this section of the *Notes.*

SYMBOLS AND IMAGES

THE STONE ANGEL

The stone angel stood in the Manawaka cemetery. At the death in childbirth of Hagar's mother, Mr. Currie had bought it "in pride to mark her bones and proclaim his dynasty, as he fancied, forever and a day" (p. 3). The statue was described by Hagar as being "doubly blind", for not only were its eyes of stone; in addition, the carver had left the eyeballs blank. Further, the stone angel was an incongruous figure in the cemetery because it had been brought from Italy "at a terrible expense", and it was made of "pure white marble."

The angel was intended to mark the grave of Mrs. Currie, and yet it was in fact a startlingly unsuitable memorial for her. She would seem to have been a gentle, undemonstrative person; Hagar describes Mrs. Currie as a "feeble ghost", but herself as a "stubborn one". Thus, the expensive, ostentatious angel --- "the first, the largest, and certainly the costliest" in the Manawaka cemetery --- was hardly meant for the dead woman at all.

In fact, the angel represented the things that Mr. Currie --- and later, Hagar --- valued. It was erected in response to *his* needs, "the needs of [a] fledgling pharaoh(s) in an uncouth land." He had bought it "in pride", and not in grief. It did not express his sorrow; it was intended to "mark her bones" and to "proclaim his dynasty". The angel, then, is symbolic of his egotism and his materialism. At his own death, the same motives found expression, for he left his money to the town in order that a memorial park, perpetuating his name, would be established.

The angel is no less symbolic of Hagar. Like the angel, Hagar seems to be made of stone. Sharing her father's pride, she will not allow herself to express emotions that might be thought of as soft. For example, when her father punishes her, she is determined not to cry (pp. 9-10). Unfortunately, however, this proud strength renders her unable to express the emotions she does feel and incapable of dealing with strong emotions in others. Consequently, when her father does show tenderness, she simply feels "caged and panicky" (p. 10). Her incapacity for the expression of tenderness is seen most movingly in the last moments in the life of her brother, Dan. Realizing that Dan needs comforting love, Matt wants Hagar to wear their mother's shawl and to cradle their dying brother. Hagar is unable to do what is demanded of her:

.... all I could think of was that meek woman I'd never seen, the woman Dan was said to resemble so much and from whom he's inherited a frailty I could not help but detest, however much a part of me wanted to sympathize. To play at being her - it was beyond me.

'I can't, Matt.' I was crying, shaken by torments he never even suspected, wanting above all else to do the thing he asked, but unable to do it, unable to bend enough.   (p. 25)

The moment is a capsulated portrait of Hagar. She is never --- until her final conversation with Marvin --- able to do the tender thing that needs to be done, or to speak the gentle word that needs to be spoken. Thus, when she feels that Matt ought to be going East to school instead of herself, she says nothing (p. 42); when her flesh responds to Bram's love, she is silent (p. 81); and when her heart opens to Bram in his distress over the death of his horse, she is impassive (p. 87-88). She had never been able to 'speak the heart's truth" (p. 292). To all appearances, her heart had been stone, as hard and unyielding as the stone angel. Hagar resembles the angel in another aspect also. The angel is symbolic of the Currie family pride. It was erected in the spirit of pride, and it was the largest and costliest in the Manawaka cemetery. Hagar shared that pride, which led to hurt and tragedy. Her pride led her to resent Arlene, because she was merely the daughter of Lottie, an illegitimate child herself. Her pride blinded her to the real love that existed between John and Arlene, and set in motion the events that led to the death of the young couple. Her pride prompted her to lie about her real relationship to Bram when she applied for employment at Mr. Oatley's; her pride made her contemptuous at first of Murray Lees; her pride blinded her to the warm humanity of Mrs. Jardine, in hospital; and her pride had led her to reject Marvin coldly, because he was not the kind of son she wanted. Hagar's pride contributes to the third comparison between Hagar and the stone angel: like the angel, Hagar was blind, "unendowed with even a pretense of sight" (p. 3). In her conversation with Murray Lees, she made an observation that described well the crux of her problem: "How you see a thing - it depends which side of the fence you're on" (p. 224). Hagar's problem had been that she saw things from only one point of view - her own. The realization of that defective vision came to Hagar from time to time, as when she cursed herself for her meanness in failing to appreciate Lottie's distress (p. 212). But, in the main Hagar had remained defiantly blind to the needs and aspirations of others. As cold emotionally as the stone angel, she was also as blind as the statue, until she met Murray Lees, whose strange companionship melted the hardness and unlocked the truth that had been buried there.

BIBLICAL IMAGERY

To begin with, the name Hagar suggests immediately the story of the Hagar in the Old Testament. That Hagar was the Egyptian hand-maiden of Sarah, the wife of Abraham. Sarah found herself unable to bear a son for her husband. In desperation, she gave her maid, Hagar, to Abraham, so that the promised heir might be conceived:

> And Sarah said unto Abraham, Behold now, the Lord hath restrained me from bearing: I pray thee, go in unto my maid; it may be that I may obtain children by her. And Abraham hearkened unto the voice of Sarah...
> ... And he went in unto Hagar, and she conceived: and when she saw that she had conceived, her mistress was despised in her eyes.
> (Genesis 16, v. 2 and v. 4)

Thus, the plan did work, and was in accord with accepted custom and law. However, human emotions blighted the outcome. Hagar became disdainful of Sarah, and Sarah was jealous of Hagar. As a result, Sarah had Hagar banished to the wilderness of Shur. There, Hagar was told by God that she would bear a son who would be called Ishmael, "a wild man" whose "hand will be against every man, and every man's hand against him". She was also commanded to return to Abraham and Sarah. Hagar did return, but years later trouble erupted once more. Sarah had at last borne a son of her own, Isaac, and at the ceremony marking the weaning of Isaac, Ishmael appeared, mocking. Once more, Hagar and her son were banished, this time to the wilderness of Beersheba. In the wilderness, Hagar was overcome by despair. She thought of leaving the unruly child to die, but God intervened by providing for her and the boy a well of water. Later, Ishmael became the progenitor of twelve princes of Israel, though his descendents were always regarded in the Old Testament narrative as inferior to those of Isaac.

The parallels between the Hagar of Genesis and the Hagar of *The Stone Angel* are clear. Like the Egyptian Hagar, Margaret Laurence's Hagar is really a bondwoman. Symbolically, she becomes a housekeeper, and is well aware of the irony of her position to one of a nature such as hers. She may briefly have thought of herself as "chatelaine" when she married Bram, but the reality of her lowly position soon became obvious to her:

> The Shipley house was square and frame, two-storied, the furniture shoddy and second-hand, the kitchen reeking and stale, for no one had scoured properly there since Clara died. Yet, seeing it, I wasn't troubled in the slightest, still thinking of myself as

> chatelaine. I wonder who I imagined would do the work? I thought
> of Polacks and Galicians from the mountain, half-breeds from the
> river valley of the Wachakwa, or the daughters and spinster aunts
> of the poor, forgetting that Bram's own daughters had hired
> out whenever they could be spared, until they married very young
> and gained a permanent employment.   (pp. 50-51)

However, the enslavement wrought by physical circumstances is only a
sign of the real bondage of Hagar. She is not free in spirit. As she
realizes herself, she had always been a captive spirit: "I was alone,
never anything else, and never free, for I carried my chains within me,
and they spread out from me and shackled all I touched" (p. 292).
Thus, though she possessed a passionate, sensuous nature and was able
to appreciate colours and sights and sounds (p. 4-5, p. 15, p.22, p.29),
she was chained and restrained by her concentration on appearances.
Even as an old woman, the appearance of things is a dominant element
in her experience, for she behaves differently when she has an
audience: " ...and of course I'm all right, perfectly all right, as I always
am when I haven't got an audience" (p. 33). Similarly, as a young
woman she had found herself responding to Bram sexually. Her "blood
and vitals" rose to meet his (p. 81). But, characteristically, she
imprisoned her response. She never let Bram know of it; she "made
certain that the trembling was all inner." Her control became, in fact, a
source of pride: "I prided myself upon keeping my pride intact, like
some maidenhead" (p. 81). She became, then, a slave to her own emot-
ional reticence, whose source was a stubborn pride in appearances and
status.

Like the Egyptian Hagar also, Hagar of Manawaka was a
creature of the wilderness. Like a pharaoh's daughter (p. 3), she left the
prosperity of her father's house for the wilderness of the Shipley place,
a farm that was a desert of vain, fitful hopes:

> ... We had precious little money - better, he thought, to spend it
> on his schemes. Honey, it was once. We would surely make our
> fortunes. Didn't the white and yellow clover teem all around?
> It did, but something else grew as well, some poisonous flower
> we never saw, hidden perhaps from the daylight, shielded by fox-
> tails that waved their barbed furry brushes in his pastures, or con-
> cealed by the reeds around the yellow-scummed slough, some
> blossom of burdock or nightshade, siren-scented to bees, no
> doubt, and deadly. His damned bees sickened and for the most
> part died, looking like scattered handfuls of shriveled raisins in the
> hives.   (pp. 56-57)

Its true nature is seen most vividly when the great drought visits the
prairies. At that time, Hagar revisited Manawaka in response to
Bram's illness. She found the colourful flowers she had planted in
defiance of the encroaching wilderness of the farm now dried and

lifeless, and in the rippling dust the Shipley place, decaying and neglected, was desert-like:

> ... the rusty machinery stood like aged bodies gradually expiring from exposure, ribs turned to the sun. The leaves of my lilac bushes were burned yellow, and the branches snapped if you touched them. The house had never been anything but gray, so it wasn't any different now, except that the front porch, which had been made of green lumer when the house was built and had been warping for years, now had been given a final pliers twist by frost and wore a caved-in look, like toothless jaws. (p. 169)

Unlike the Hagar of the Old Testament, however, the Hagar of the novel did not encounter a theophany at the Shipley place. There was no comforting assurance of divine grace for her. Thus, when Bram disgraced her in her father's old store (p. 135), she reached her decision to leave her husband. Like the handmaiden of old, she took her son, John with her. Her flight proved to be fruitless. The coast offered only an appearance of new life. True, the desert was left behind, but it was exchanged only for the artificiality of Mr. Oatley's garden. Life there was as artificial as Mr. Oatley's habit of praising the great classics of literature and then indulging in his favourite reading --- detective stories! It was not a time of fruitful harvesting. Life there, in Hagar's own opinion was "becalmed" (p. 160), and the term echoes the death-in-life experience of Coleridge's Ancient Mariner, with whom she compares herself later (p. 186).

At that point in the narrative, the parallel with the Old Testament Hagar is deepened. Just as that Hagar learned in the wilderness that her son was to have a wild nature, so on the coast Hagar discovers John's true character. She ignores the evidence of what John really is, overlooking the lies and deceptions, evading the evidence of his too-easy charm, and ignoring his failures at work, which should have reminded her of Bram. But the identification with Bram becomes clear on her return to Manawaka, when she sees John dressed in Bram's clothes. The moment is clearly symbolic:

> ... He wore an old pair of Bram's overalls, so stiff with dirt they'd have stood alone. He'd lost so much weight. His face was like a skull's and yet he grinned as though it pleased him no end to look that way.
>
> 'Welcome to your castle,' he said, and made a bow.
>
> I looked at him shrewdly *and wondered why I hadn't noticed before.* (pp. 170-171. Italics added)

What Hagar had not chosen to notice before was the similarity between John and Bram, which was emphasized by his complete care of his father (p. 172). Hagar's insight is confirmed later on the visit to the cemetery. On that occasion, the stone angel is seen to have been toppled. There is little doubt that John had been responsible for the small act of desecration. Like his father's urinating on the steps of Mr. Currie's store (p. 115), John action had no doubt been an expression of his contempt for the values cherished by the Curries and their daughter, Hagar. Yet, as Hagar set John to the task of righting the angel, she still hoped that her son might be a faithful son, like the Jacob of the Old Testament. But she knew in that moment the vanity of her hopes:

> I wish he could have looked like Jacob then, wrestling with the angel and besting it, wringing a blessing from it with his might. But no. He sweated and grunted angrily. His feet slipped and he hit his forehead on a marble ear, and swore. (p. 179)

The truth which the wilderness revealed to Hagar was not a truth that she welcomed. The theophany had come, but it had come with bitter irony. There is no less irony in the results of Hagar's second wilderness experience, which is represented by her sojourn at Shadow Point. From that experience, Hagar saw at last that she had misjudged Marvin. He, not John, was the son of promise; he, not John, was Jacob:

> I stare at him. Then, quite unexpectedly, he reaches for my hand and holds it tightly.
> Now it seems to me he is truly Jacob, gripping with all his strength, and bargaining. *I will not let thee go, except thou bless me.* And I see I am thus strangely cast, and perhaps have been so from the beginning, and can only release myself by releasing him...
> "You've not been cranky, Marvin. You've been good to me, always. A better son than John."

Hagar's words are untruthful, but they spring from a true recognition of Marvin's worth. Thus they express the illumination and wisdom that had at last come to her through the wilderness. Hagar had produced her Ishmael, the wild one whose life had been a bane, but she had also produced her own faithful son, a Jacob who was a blessed descendent of Isaac.

There is a further parallel between the Hagar of the Old Testament and Margaret Laurence's Hagar. This aspect can be understood most clearly and justified by an examination of the name 'Hagar'. The origins of the name are obscure, but semantically it would seem to have some connection with the verb "to flee." Thus, for example, the famous flight of the prophet Mohammed from the city of Mecca (June, 622) is known as the "hegira", and all dates in Islam are identified by their relationship to this flight; in the western world, Moslem dates are usually accompanied by the initials A.H., meaning "After the Hegira." The Old Testament Hagar, true to her name, undertook two major flights from Abraham and Isaac. As has been pointed out elsewhere in these *Notes* (see STRUCTURE), Hagar of Manawaka undertook two major flights also. On the first occasion, she fled from the Shipley place to the coast, taking her son with her. On the second occasion, she fled from Marvin and Doris. The second flight resulted eventually in what might be described as her theophany experience, when, visited by Mr. Troy in hospital, she found herself able to rejoice.

Further, in more general terms, the development of Hagar's character takes on aspects of a religious pattern. Again, this concept is explored in detail in another section of these *Notes* (see STRUCTURE). There is no exact allegory here, along the lines of Bunyan's *Pilgrim's Progress*. But Hagar does appear to experience an epiphany which is given a religious context, when Mr. Troy's singing of a hymn awakens her to the missing element in her life. Also, her grasping of the glass at the end of the novel, with all its connotations of water as the symbolic quencher of spiritual thirst, does seem to suggest that Hagar has reached at last some kind of understanding and some kind of peace. It is true that in some ways she is unrepentant to the end. She is still rude and demanding towards Doris. Stubborn as ever, she is still able to declare, "I'll drink from this glass, or spill it, just as I choose" (p. 308). But Hagar has shown a tenderness which she could not bring herself to express previously. She has wept, whereas she had not wept over the death of Bram or the death of John. She has also admitted the wrongness of her actions towards John and Arlene. Above all, perhaps, she has been able to give Marvin the blessing which he craved all of his life. The redemptive pattern, then, is not a fixed and exact correspondence with the usual Christian pattern, but nonetheless it is there as a vital and discernible aspect of the novel.

FLOWER IMAGERY

There are two main kinds of flowers mentioned in *The Stone Angel,* wild flowers and cultivated flowers. The two are pictured vividly in an early scene in the novel. Hagar recalls walking in the cemetery as a little girl. Her recollections are worth quoting at length, because they set the pattern for the interpretation of the flower imagery in the novel:

> In summer the cemetery was rich and thick as syrup with the funeral-parlor perfume of the planted peonies, dark crimson and wallpaper pink, the pompous blossoms hanging leadenly, too heavy for their light stems, bowed down with the weight of themselves and the weight of the rain, infested with upstart ants that sauntered through the plush petals as though to the manner born.
> I used to walk there often when I was a girl. There could not have been many places to walk primly in those days on paths, where white kid boots and dangling skirts would not be torn by thistles or put in unseemly disarray. How anxious I was to be neat

and orderly, imagining life had been created only to celebrate tidiness, like prissy Pippa as she passed. But sometimes through the hot rush of disrespectful wind that shook the scrub oak and the coarse couchgrass encroaching upon the dutifully cared-for habitations of the dead, the scent of the cowslips would rise momentarily. They were tough-rooted, these wild and gaudy flowers, and although they were held back at the cemetery's edge, torn out by loving relatives determined to keep the plots clear and clearly civilized, for a second or two a person walking there could catch the faint, musky, dust-tinged smell of things that grew untended, and had grown always, before the portly peonies and the angels with rigid wings, when the prairie bluffs were walked through only by Cree with enigmatic faces and greasy hair. (pp. 4-5)

What is presented here is not only the contrast between two kinds of flowers, the cultivated and the wild, but also the contrast between two responses to life, the calculated and the spontaneous. The contrast is made clearer by the reflections of Hagar, which follow. She declares that now, in her old age, each day has "a rarity" for her, so that "I could put it in a vase and admire it, like the first dandelions, and we would forget their weediness and marvel that they were there at all." That expresses the natural response to natural things. With the quality of spontaneous response, each day becomes a rarity, an expression of the celebration of what is natural and precious. Immediately, however, Hagar indicates the attitude that is more commonly adopted: "But one dissembles, usually, for the sake of such people as Marvin, who is somehow comforted by the picture of old ladies feeding like docile rabbits on the lettuce leaves of other times, other manners." This dissembling, we see as the novel unfolds, is actually one of Hagar's grave defects. She responds naturally, but she can never express that naturalness. In her concern for appearances, she continually masks the natural, scorning it as weakness.

But the connotations associated with the cultivated flowers are ominous. They have a "funeral-parlour perfume", reminiscent of death, and they are "pompous" in their empty showiness. They speak of empty and sterile life that vainly tries to do battle with the desert-like prairie. Superficially, Hagar is aware of the connotations as she dabs eau de Cologne on her wrists, but --- ironically --- she is unaware of the application of the connotations to her own life:

> ... It is *Lily of the Valley*. I do not blame her Tina for this choice, nor do I think it was due to any tactlessness on her part. I would not expect her to know that the lilies of the valley, so white and almost too strongly sweet, were the flowers we used to weave into the wreaths for the dead. (p. 33)

This blindness of Hagar to the stifling artificiality that she brings to her own life and to the lives of those around her can be discerned in her wedding to Bram Shipley. She was attracted to him by the strangest of natural signs, among them the "crescents of ingrown earth" in his fingernails. Following her marriage, as she drives with him to the Shipley place, she is alive to the sights and sounds of the natural fruitfulness of the earth, for the "poplar bluffs had budded with sticky leaves, and the frogs had come back to the sloughs and sang like choruses of angels with sore throats, and the marsh marigolds were opening like shavings of sun on the brown river where the tadpoles danced" (p. 50). However, Hagar herself was not akin to nature. She was not really in tune with the impulses of spring, so that she might bring to the marriage a spontaneous and loving heart. She was in a dream world. She saw herself as "chatelaine", and her dominant motive became that of changing her husband by the addition of a veneer of manners.

Hence, even Hagar's beloved lilacs act as an ironic image, underscoring the lack of the spontaneous and the natural in her own life. The lilacs at the Shipley place were rich in their beauty and sensuous in their perfume, but they grew "with no care given them" (p. 29), just as Hagar gave no care to what was natural in her own life. Thus it is fitting that the failure of Hagar's efforts should be illustrated by the death of her cultivated flowers in the time of drought:

> ... My marigolds were a dead loss by this time, of course. I'd planted them behind the house to use as cutting flowers and they'd kept on seeding themselves, but now only a few wizened ones remained, small unexpected dabs of orange among the choking weeds, dry sheepfoot and thistle. The sunflowers had risen beside the barn as always, fed by the melting snow in spring, but they'd had no other water this year - their tall stalks were hollow and brown, and the heavy heads hung over, the segments empty as unfilled honeycombs, for the petals had fallen and the centers had dried before the seeds could form. (p. 169)

Hagar's efforts at artificiality had brought only sterility, the sterility of which she would become aware only in her very old age.

Significantly, when Hagar began to be aware of the wrong impulses in her life, she cast aside the artificial, represented by the artificial flowers in her hat. At Shadow Point, in a moment possessed of grotesquely comic overtones, she plucked the flowers from her hat and replaced them with June bugs. It was a symbolic gesture, foreshadowing the epiphany to come.

72

THEMES

In a sense, *The Stone Angel* is a novel whose main theme is the *futility of escape.* Sharply etched against the background of the dry, unyielding prairies, its characters seem to twist and turn and manoeuvre to evade the destiny that has been thrust upon them. They seek to escape --- from family influences, from their own sense of emptiness, from the destiny that faces them implacably --- but their efforts, however valiant or however pathetic, are doomed to failure.

Mr. Currie is a vivid example of a man imprisoned in his own life. He inherited a "good family", but no money. His father was Sir Daniel Currie, a former military man who had served with distinction in India, and who had become a silk importer, ending his days in bankruptcy. He passed to his son a blessing and a curse. The blessing was the Currie name with all its suggestions of glory: they were Highland Scots, sept of the Clanranald MacDonalds, marching to their own pipe music, and with their own family motto, *Gainsay Who Dare.* But the blessing was also a curse. For Mr. Currie, Hagar's father, was deluded by the past glory of the family. He himself was a self-made man. He had left Scotland as a young man and come to "the bald-headed prairie", becoming a storekeeper and a leading citizen in Manawaka. However, the very qualities that had led to his material success blighted his life as a human being. His pride in his prosperity and in his position made his life a desert. It led him to erect the stone angel in the Manawaka cemetery, an absurd, almost grotesque, monument to a wife who had been shy and timid. More than a memorial, it was his proclamation of success, proclaiming him as 'a fledgling pharaoh in an uncouth land.' The same attitude dominated his religious life. He observed his religious duties scrupulously --- he never missed a Sunday service, and he never missed saying grace at meals. But he was fiercely proud of his position in the congregation, and it was a position proclaimed in materialistic terms:

> "On this great day," the Reverend Dougall MacCulloch said feelingly, "we have to give special thanks to those of our congregation whose generosity and Christian contributions have made our new church possible."
> He called them off, the names, like an honor roll. Luke McVitie, lawyer. Jason Currie, businessman. Freeman McKendrick, bank manager. Burns MacIntosh, farmer. Rab Fraser, farmer.
> Father sat with modestly bowed head, but turned to me and whispered very low:
> "I and Luke McVitie must've given the most, as he called our names first." (p. 16)

With such blinding pride, it is scarcely surprising that Mr. Currie's relationships with others were sterile. Auntie Doll, presumably the sister of his widow, kept house for him for years, but he did not marry her; "... he could never have brought himself to marry his house-keeper" (p. 17). Further, he did not understand the personalities of his own sons. He shattered the dreams of Matt, who pathetically and feverishly collected coins in order to provide for college and a future; "Matt," he declared, "can learn all he needs right here, if he's minded to do so" (p. 42). Mr. Currie had "small patience" with his delicate second son, Dan, who died tended only by the love of Matt. Finally, to Hagar Mr. Currie gave the worst legacy of all --- the pride that was her wilderness. It was the same pride that had imprisoned him all of his life and had made him unable to respond to the feelings of love that he had, for example, for Lottie's mother; it was the pride which made him dis-own the grandsons he had through Hagar, and which finally expressed itself in the memorial park that bore his name.

Bram Shipley, in his own way, was no less a prisoner. Regarded as lazy and good-for-nothing, he remained fiercely true to his reputation. Just as Mr. Currie had proclaimed his materialistic pride, so Bram Shipley proclaimed his worthlessness. He asserted his contempt for Mr. Currie's values by urinating on the steps of Currie's store, and, confronted by the social pretensions of Charlotte Tappen, he "hugged surliness like a winter coat around him" (p. 70). And yet, in his own way, he had the capacity for love and affection. With Hagar as his wife, that capacity was never realized. The potential and tragedy of their relationship is perhaps most clearly seen in the moment when they are alone together for the first time, following their wedding:

> ... when we entered, Bram handed me a cut-glass decanter with a silver top.
> "This here's for you, Hagar."
> I took it so casually, and laid it aside, and thought no more about it. He picked it up in his hands and turned it around. For a moment I thought he meant to break it, and for the life of me I couldn't see why. Then he laughed and set it down and came close to me.
> "Let's see what you look like under all that rig-out, Hagar."
>
> (p. 51)

Bram's gift was a gift of love. Characteristically avoiding any show of emotion, Hagar treated it "casually." Bram was hurt, as his thoughtful handling of the gift shows. In his hurt, he reverted to type. He acted in a manner expected of him. Harshly and uncouthly, he bade Hagar to take off her clothes so that she might perform her wifely duties. The scene is a little cameo of the central tragedy of the novel. It is the tragedy of potential which is never realized, of love that is never

74

uttered, of people who imprison themselves in the roles expected of them.

Hagar herself is, of course, the most vivid example of the captive who wishes to escape from the prison of her own attitudes. She wishes, in Daniel's dying moments, to express her love by playing the part of her dead mother, but she could not bring herself to be like "that meek woman". In response to Bram's love, she felt her body rising to meet his, but she refused to "betray" herself, "like a heedless and compelled maple after winter" (p. 81). As a child, Marvin sought love and approval from his mother. He would hang around the kitchen, after doing little chores for, awaiting her approval. But Hagar never spoke the words he wanted to hear (p. 113). Not until Mr. Troy's moving singing of the hymn in hospital was Hagar set free from the captivity forged by her pride; only then were the chains loosed, so that she was able to give Marvin the blessing he had sought throughout his life.

Thus, even physical escape from Manawaka serves no purpose. Hagar flees to Vancouver and becomes housekeeper for Mr. Oatley. In the end, however, she must return. She returns pathetically unchanged and is unable to affect any change in her relationship with the dying Bram. Her love had been unspoken and unexpressed, and the signs of it --- their physical intimacy --- is now a thing of the past. Bram does not even recognize her. In contrast, Marvin did at last make his peace with his father; he entered his father's room at night to say that he was sorry. Hagar wished to do what Marvin had done --- "to say even once what Marvin had said" (p. 183) --- but she could not. She was still the prisoner of her self. Similarly, John was unable to escape from Manawaka. He went with Hagar to the coast, but he returned. His act was purely voluntary. Caught in the clash between his father and his mother, he could not evade his destiny. He returned to become a second Bram. Nor could Marvin escape. He had left at the age of seventeen to fight his own battles, but the old life followed him. In his old age, Manawaka came to reside with him, in the person of his mother. With her mementoes and memories of Manawaka, she was the embodiment of the past that he could not cast aside. He is unwilling to abandon that past, by sending Hagar to Silverthreads. He seeks peace and quiet in his den, but the peace that he needs must come from Hagar. Manawaka, and all that it has meant in his life, must be wrestled with, so that finally a blessing must come from it. The blessing does come at last. Significantly, however, that blessing takes the form of a lie. Marvin is told that he has been a better son than John, but Hagar does not really mean what she says. Able to understand at last that love may be expressed in a curious fashion, she speaks the words which are needed, freeing both herself and Marvin.

The Stone Angel breathes an atmosphere of tragic futility. Locked in the prison of their own attitudes and emotions, the characters fail to communicate with one another meaningfully. Like the cultivated flowers in the cemetery and around the Shipley place, they seek desperately to keep at bay the threat of the wild life of the prairies. Their success in much of the novel is the measure of their tragedy.

OTHER WORKS

THE FIRE-DWELLERS

The central character in this novel is Stacey Cameron, a thirty-nine year-old housewife with four children. She is a confused and despondent woman, worried about trivialities such as the fat that the years have added to her hips, and worried about her own sense of isolation even in the middle of a family. She looks out upon the world and is overcome by a sense of futility. Much of the dialogue in the novel mirrors that sense of futility. For example, her conversations with her husband, Mac, who is a salesman struggling to provide for his family, are curiously inconclusive. Their words fail to express what is really felt or what each needs to utter. Like the existentialist tramps in Samuel Beckett's *Waiting for Godot*, Stacey and Mac talk in a manner that reminds one of a tennis game, with the ball going back and forth over the net and occasionally being missed by one of the pair:

> Mac
> What now for God's sake
> What do you think, I mean, in yourself?
> What do you mean what do I think in myself?
> Just what do you *think*?
> What do you *mean*, what do I think? Like What?
> Well, I mean
> Just what *do* you mean, Stacey?
> I guess the product's pretty good, eh?
> I told you
> What about - I mean, what do you think of Thor?
> I think he's a guy with drive.
> I think he's bat-winged Mephistopheles.
> You must be out of your mind.
> Are you levelling with me, Mac?
> For heaven's sake. What is there to level *about*?
> Why don't you say what you mean, just once? Why not? Look, I *know*.
> You do, eh? You really think you do?   (p. 44)

This inability to communicate meaningfully with others is not a problem peculiar to Stacey alone. All of the characters in the novel --- with the exception of Luke Venturi, Stacey's lover --- have a similar problem. They are all, as it were, prisoners of their own flesh and of their own minds. Within the walls of the self, emotions are stirred and thoughts cascade, but they find no meaningful expression. Thus, in a sense Stacey's two-year-old daughter, Jen, is a symbolic representation of the condition that haunts everyone: she cannot talk. For this reason, the people in the book exist in relationships that are unfulfilling, suffocating the vibrant life of the self that continues to exist within its cell. For example, Bertha Garvey, sixtyish, with "eyes always a little worried behind up-curled green-framed glasses", is married to a retired accountant, Julian, who is "meticulous-mannered with everyone else, but crabby with Bertha." Aware of Bertha's suffocation at the hands of Julian, Stacey wonders what dreams Bertha has as compensation for the realities of her life: "What does Bertha concoct for her personal theater? The lumberjack she never married, the one who would have loved her with perfect admiration just as she is?" (p. 274) Tess and Jake Fogler, Stacey's neighbours, are no better. Jake is "a radio actor who is fond of talking about the breakdown of verbal communications and the problems of semantics in mass media" (p. 82). Yet the lack of communication between himself and Tess is remarkable and, ultimately, tragic. They have no children, and Tess has believed that Jake did not want children; he thought that she did not want children because she was "damn scared" (p. 272). In addition, Tess has believed that Jake considered her to be stupid. He has thus spent his life egotistically indulging in his moods, and she has spent her days trying to look more beautiful and spending money on knickknacks. Thus, bored with her life and anxious about her relationship with her husband, Tess attempts suicide. Naturally, Jake is completely bewildered by her act. He cannot understand it at all, as his conversation with Stacey reveals:

> ... His voice is only pain and bewilderment.
> Yes but why? Why would she? What's the matter with her? What did I do wrong? Was it me? What was it?
> I don't know
> - I don't know and I do know. Dog eat dog and fish eat fish. How many things added up? But I didn't get the message either. Why didn't I? I always envied her for being so glamorous. I couldn't see anything else.
> Jake   I'm so damn sorry   I did know she was upset sometimes and I might have tried   but I didn't
> You shouldn't think that way, Stacey. It was me. I guess. But what did I do or not do? (p. 271)

Not even Mac's father, Matthew, the retired minister, can lay claim to a meaningful bond with others. Suffering from glaucoma, he has stumbled and fallen while visiting his son's home. Though she has never been able to be frank with him, Stacey insists that he must come to live with Mac and herself. Matthew is hesitant to accept the invitation, for, "always so neat and so proud", he feels that he cannot impose upon her. His real reason for hesitation, however, is his son. Matthew does not feel that he 'did very well by Mac' when he was a boy. He was aware, he explains to Stacey, of the unfair expectations held of a minister's son, but he had said nothing of the problems to Mac. He had wanted his son to "grow up with some strong background of faith", but his son had not. For this, the father blamed himself. "Perhaps," he speculates, "there is something contagious about doubt", and his son, he declares, "must have known all along about that essential flaw" in his father. Stacey's reply is a telling one: Mac would have been relieved if he'd known you weren't always certain. But he didn't know" (p. 283). Once again, then, in the relationship between Mac and his father, it is evident that the silence imposed upon feeling has wrought its havoc in human lives. The total incapacity to relate is illustrated most vividly and horribly in Mac's friend, Buckle. A truck driver, his life is bound to his hours on the road. His wife has left him some time previously, and Stacey discovers the reason for her desertion when, overcome by her feelings of isolation, she prepares to have sexual relations with Buckle. Horrifyingly, she learns that he does not want her affection or her caresses; he can only achieve sexual satisfaction by masturbating himself in the presence of a woman.

The people in the novel are thus seen to be isolated beings, who suffer the torments of existence alone. In view of this, it is not surprising that the common metaphor for life in the novel is that of hell. Fire imagery pervades the book. At night, Stacey drives in the city "along streets now inhabited only by the eternal flames of the neon forest fires" (p. 167), as though, fleeing from her house, she is making her way through some Dante-like Inferno. The flames of hell are a repeated *motif*, usually bursting in upon domestic life with the voice of a television newscaster:

> EVER-OPEN EYE. BOUGAINVILLAEA BURGEONING, EDGING STREETS WHERE BEGGARS SQUAT IN THE DUST. A MAN BURNING. HIS FACE CANNOT BE SEEN. HE LIES STILL, PERHAPS ALREADY DEAD. FLAMES LEAP AND QUIVER FROM HIS BLACKENED ROBE LIKE EXCITED CHILDREN OF HELL. VOICE: TODAY ANOTHER BUDDHIST MONK SET FIRE TO HIMSELF IN PROTEST AGAINST THE WARIN   (p. 125)

The scenario may actually depict some distant scene in the remote Far East, but the setting is without doubt the city in which Stacy lives and the kind of life which she and others find themselves leading. For the fires are everywhere. They are inside tortured souls, who feel passionately but talk listlessly or seldom. They are within relationships that sterilize and destroy vitality. They are in the tormenting anxiety about death and injury that Stacey often fears for her children. In all their savage mockery, they are expressed in the epigraph to the novel:

> Ladybird, ladybird,
> Fly away home;
> Your house is on fire,
> Your children are gone.

Yet, in spite of everything, Stacey lives defiantly. She may be marked by the painful stigmata of burns on her hand (p. 140), burns which suggest the sufferings of a Christ, but she clings to her sense of life. "I'm Stacey Cameron," she affirms, "and I still love to dance" (p. 134). She is tortured by visions of what might have been as she struggles to make the connection between the image of herself in youth and the reality of what she is at thirty-nine. She knows that she has delivered herself into the hands of lies and trivialities, "the tiredness we never knew about until it had taken up permanent residence inside our arteries" (p. 23); she is so aware that sometimes she wonders if she really exists (p. 11). Nevertheless, there is a stubbornness within her which seeks release; there is a capacity for living which struggles for expression. She looks doggedly for some expression of herself:

> ... But how is it I can feel as well that I'm spending my life in one unbroken series of trivialities? The kids don't belong to me. They belong to themselves. It would be nice to have something of my own, that's all. I can't go anywhere as myself. Only as Mac's wife or the kids' mother. (p. 95)

As a result, there is persistent imagery in the novel which stresses the contrast between what is and what appears to be. "Under this chapeau," Stacey affirms, "lurks a mermaid, a whore, a tigress" (p. 12). The mermaid imagery in particular emphasizes the rebirth theme. It is familiar imagery, of course, but nonetheless powerful and suggestive in its suggestion of the ocean as a force symbolic of rebirth and regeneration. To the biologist, it is a truism to declare that without water there is no life. To the writer in all ages, the ocean and its waters have suggested the possibilities of a life that is vital, free and meaningful. Thus, in one aspect, Stacey *is* a mermaid --- a creature of the sea and a creature of vigorous, meaningful potential. It is thus significant that Luke Venturi's pet name for Stacey is 'Mermaid'. For Stacey is potentially the mermaid, the creature of the ocean, the romantic figure evocative of a quality of life far different from that which she knows in everyday existence. She may indeed be the mother of the stereotype: teaching values in which she does not really believe and which, in part at least, she hates (p. 5); feeling herself strangely isolated in the city which is her home (p. 8); playing a game which gives her only a sense of crippling guilt (p. 71). But she *is* Stacey Cameron.

The problem lies in the reconciliation of the two roles: Stacey as mermaid and Stacey the thirty-nine year-old drab. Thus, the sea imagery has two sides to it. On the one hand, the mermaid imagery suggests a different quality of life, a quality inherent in her initial escape from the prairies and its suffocating environment, where "all the trains ever said was, Get on your way, somewhere, just so something will happen, get up and get out of this town" (p. 33). On the other hand, the sea is fraught with dangers. Not only may it suggest possibilities of freedom and vigour; it may also suggest death and suffocation:

> Everything drifts. Everything is slowly swirling, philosophies
> tangled with grocery lists, unreal-real anxieties like rose thorns
> waiting to tear the uncertain flesh, nonentities of thought floating
> like plankton, green and orange particles, seaweed - lots of that,
> dark purple and waving, sharks with fins like cutlasses, herself
> held underwater by her hair, snared around auburn-rusted anchor
> chains.

Fittingly, at the ocean --- the beach home of Luke Venturi --- Stacey
finds the answer for which she has been looking. There, she is able to
find herself, as Luke observes that "I can just about make you out in
there, but miniature, like looking through the wrong end of a telescope" (p. 181). Her life, Stacey discovers, is revealed in the pattern
that has been set. She *is* the woman she has become and, as her dialogue with Luke reveals, the mould cannot be changed by thoughts of
what might have been:

> You want to sleep with me, all night, so why don't you?
> I can't. I can't stay away all night. It's not possible.
> You're a strange woman.
> That's not being strange. The other would be
> Okay. That's your problem, I guess.
> She dresses swiftly, and by the time she has her hair combed,
> Luke is also dressed and standing by the door. He kisses her
> lightly.
> So long, then. Stacey.
> - I actually want to thank him. I want to explain myself to him,
> make myself real to him. I want to say - look, this is what I'm like.
> (p. 204)

The answer to the human problem thus becomes --- strangely,
though nonetheless magnificently --- survival. It is an answer which
harks back to an earlier experience of Stacey's, when she watched a
sea-gull at the shore:

> At the beach, once. Stacey watching a gull repeatedly dropping a
> closed clamshell from a great height. Finally the shell cracked on a
> rock, and the bird landed and calmly fed. Stacey had to admire
> such a simple knowledge of survival. (p. 10)

In the light of this truth that life is simply enduring, that life goes on,
that life *is* its humdrum reality, Stacey is able to put her brief affair
with Luke in perspective. It was an oasis in the desert of life. It offered
refreshment and hope, if even for only a few brief moments. It had
given the reassurance of what was needed to confront reality, but it had
been no more than that:

> ... Luke? I couldn't let you see me. All right - you showed me
> where I belonged, when you said, *What can't you leave*? I guess I

should be grateful. I *am* grateful. Maybe not for that, so much. I guess I knew it anyway. For the way you talked to me and held me for a while - that's why I'm grateful. I said unspokenly *Help* and you didn't turn away. You faced me and touched me. You were gently. You needn't have been, but you were, and that I won't forget or cease to be glad for. Even if you'd been older, or I'd been younger and free, it wouldn't have turned out any simpler with you than it is with Mac. I didn't see that at one time, but I see it now.

(pp. 277-278)

Stacey had learned of the stubbornness of human survival. In spite of the frustrations, in spite of the doomed dreams, in spite of the pain of solitude, human beings endured and lived on. That was the human bond which united all of them --- Mac, herself, and the children. With a few more years of life, she would have "a hide like a rhinoceros" (p. 285). Mac was much stronger than he thought he was. The children were much stronger than they thought they were. Even Stacey was probably much stronger than she conceived herself as being.

True, the epiphany has its dark aspects. The insight does not solve problems. As Stacey observes, "We are ourselves and we are sure as hell not going to undergo some total transformation at this point" (p. 289). But it is a positive affirmation, and it appears to achieve positive results in the life of Stacey Cameron. In her conversation with Mac (pp. 257-258), she comes closer to him than she has ever been before. She also draws closer to her own daughter, Katie (p. 209). She even finds herself, finally, able to call Matthew 'Dad'. And at the end, there is even a suggestion of peace:

… The house is quiet. The kids are asleep. Downstairs in the ex-study, Matthew has been asleep for hours, or if not asleep, meditating. Beside her, she can already hear the steady breathing that means Mac is asleep. Temporarily, they are all more or less okay.

She feels the city receding as she slides into sleep. Will it return tomorrow? (p. 308)

The rub, of course, lies in the final question, "Will it return tomorrow?" It will return tomorrow. The reality will be there, in spite of human dreams and aspirations. The human condition is fixed and unalterable, and the best that human beings can do is to cherish their dreams and fantasies:

- I was wrong to think of the trap as the four walls. It's the world. The truth is that I haven't been Stacey Cameron for one hell of a long time now. Although in some ways I'll always be her, because that's how I started out. But from now on, the dancing goes on only in my head. (p. 303)

The Fire-Dwellers is thus a fascinating study of a genuine human problem. It probes that problem of identity which has become a characteristic of the twentieth-century, with its preoccupation with the reality of the self in relation to others. It offers no easy solution, but it is, in a very special sense, an optimistic novel. Though it presents no climactic panacea, it does affirm the magnificence of human persistence and human endurance. The gods, then, may play their vicious games with humans, against whom the dice of fate may be heavily loaded, but the human beings remain, having learned the lesson, at once both simple and complex, of survival. As Stacey might express it, we are probably all a lot stronger than we think we are.

Margaret Laurence's narrative techniques in *The Fire-Dwellers* are a refinement of the methods in *The Stone Angel*. In this later novel, the techniques are more complex. The narrative offers an intriguing compound, made up of Stacey Cameron's thoughts, her fantasies, her memories, her actual conversations with others, news from radio and television, and third-person commentary. The melange is successful, for the seemingly inconsequential events of the novel, which largely revolve around Stacey's drab existence, come together to compose a picture that is heavy with a sense of the human tragedy. Thus, the various elements of the narrative are not unrelated. The narrator's comments, for example, frequently show the difference between the Stacey revealed in her own fantasy world and the Stacey seen by those around her. The contrast between what Stacey thinks as she talks and what she actually says to others accomplishes the same purpose. The result is an emphasis upon the complexity of an apparently ordinary person. In Stacey, a drab, middle-aged, undistinguished housewife, the dreams of all human beings come to life, and the one reality --- life itself --- is confronted nobly.

A BIRD IN THE HOUSE (1974)

This volume is not a novel. It is a collection of short stories published over the years since 1963 in various magazines.

The stories, no matter what their intrinsic value, provide an excellent prologue to Margaret Laurence's novels, and before engaging in close study of *The Stone Angel, The Fire-Dwellers* and *A Jest of God*, the reader would be well advised to read *A Bird in the House*. Many of the themes with which Margaret Laurence grapples and many of the characters whom she presents appear in basic form in the short stories. They are thus a good introduction to what may be called Margaret Laurence's archetypes.

To begin with, the stories are set in the fictitious town of Manawaka, so familiar to the readers of the novel. Hagar Shipley, of *The Stone Angel*, was born there and married there, and in a sense her whole life was an attempt to escape the town and all that it had meant. Similarly, Stacey Cameron, in *The Fire-Dwellers*, returns repeatedly to memories of Manawaka, recapturing the experiences which had shaped her life and personality and seeking to establish the connection between her youth and her present middle-age. Further, the characters in the novels and the short stories have links with one another in a different way. For example, Grandfather Connor, in *A Bird in the House*, is the grim patriarchal figure, rigidly controlled in emotions and fiercely proud in materialism, who is embodied in the character of Mr. Currie, Hagar's father, in *The Stone Angel*. In addition, the stay-at-home spinster appears in several forms in Margaret Laurence's work. In *The Stone Angel*, she is bitingly mocked in the person of Regina Weese; in *A Bird in the House*, she is sympathetically portrayed in Aunt Edna; and in *The Fire-Dwellers*, there are suggestions of the archetypal figure in the shadowy presence of Rachel, Stacey's sister. Moreover, the characters are engaged in similar struggles. *The Stone Angel* is, in some ways, a novel which concentrates on the need for escape from all that Manawaka has meant. Stacey Cameron, hearing the insistent whispering of the trains --- "Get on your way, somewhere, just so something will happen, get up and get out of this town" --- ponders the problem of what it is that she is seeking to escape. In the same way, Vanessa, in *A Bird in the House*, comes to terms with the past and its people; she *does* escape, though her victory is heavy with irony:

> I parked the car beside the Brick House. The caragana hedge was unruly. No one had trimmed it properly that summer. The house had been lived in by strangers for a long time. I had not thought it would hurt me to see it in other hands, but it did. I wanted to tell them to trim their hedges, to repaint the window-frames, to pay heed to repairs. I had feared and fought the old man, yet he proclaimed himself in my veins. (p. 207)

Quite apart from their own merits, then, the short stories are important for their contribution to the context of Margaret Laurence's Canadian novels. For this reason, in the *Notes* each story will be briefly presented and analyzed, concentrating on aspects which are obviously significant in relation to *The Stone Angel* and *The Fire-Dwellers*.

The dominant figure in "The Sound of Singing", the first story, is Grandfather Connor, Vanessa's maternal grandfather. He is, first and foremost, a man who has achieved success by his own industry. Thus, he has built the first brick house in Manawaka, "part dwelling place and part massive monument". Moreover, he is overtly proud of his success, declaring, " ... I done a sight better than I would've done if I'd sat at home like some fellows I could mention, just waiting for the business to come to me." As a result, his values are the same as those cherished by Jason Currie: industry and resourcefulness are seen as basic virtues, for if a man does not achieve prosperity, the fault can be blamed upon his own laziness. Not surprisingly, Mr. Connor ruled his household with a firm hand. No one was permitted to smoke in his presence; his two daughters, Edna and Vanessa's mother, had to seek what freedom they could in whispered conversations in the kitchen; apart from one small act of independence in making her husband call back his brother with whom he had quarrelled, Mrs. Connor accepts her husband's dominance. The situation is symbolized by the caged pet bird that Grandmother Connor keeps. Vanessa asks her whether the bird minded being there; the reply is significant: "... she shook her head and said no, it had been there always and wouldn't know what to do with itself outside". The creature is, then, a picture of the family entrapment that is a feature of Margaret Laurence's Canadian novels. Not surprisingly, along with this sense of a closed world, there are hints of the familiar escape theme. The child Vanessa scribbles melodramatic adventure stories. The title of the short story refers to the singing of Irish songs by Uncle Dan, who is the complete antithesis of his brother, Timothy Connor. Unsuccessful in material terms, Dan appears in the story as an attractive, free spirit. Consequently, when at the end Vanessa, at her grandmother's bidding, runs after Dan to bring him back to the house, it is almost as though she is chasing a whole, elusive and compelling way of life: "And I ran, ran towards the sound of the singing. But he seemed a long way off now, and I wondered if I would ever catch up to him."

The Laurence archetypes are obviously established clearly in the story, and are worth noting:

--- the appearance of the dominant patriarchal figure who rules decisively in his family

--- the Manawaka stress upon the virtue of material success, which is regarded as the sign of a man's moral uprightness

--- the sense that the vitality of the life of the individual lies buried within him, and that relationships are based upon, not truth and revelation, but upon evasion and concealment

--- the atmosphere of entrapment in a whole way of life which moves inexorably in set directions

--- the suggestions of the need for escape, which is often accomplished in the fantasy life of the people who are caught in the trap of circumstances.

"To Set Our House in Order", the second story, deals with events that occurred in association with the birth of Vanessa's brother.

Because of complications, Vanessa's mother had to enter hospital two weeks before the birth, and the household was left in charge of Grandmother MacLeod, in whose home Vanessa and her parents lived.

Grandmother MacLeod is the female counterpart of the dour Scottish patriarchs of the novels. She is "steel-spined despite her apparent fragility, and her firm conviction is that "God loves Order". Thus she cannot understand, or sympathize with, her son's lack of money, even though he is a country doctor whose patients pay him in kind rather than in cash. Having money, she declares, is "mainly a question of management", and she goes on to claim, "My accounts were always in good order, and so was my house. No unexpected expenses that couldn't be met, no fruit cellar running out of preserves before the winter was over." Characteristically, she tries to pass on to Vanessa a sense of the glory of her Scottish lineage, with its gloomy mottos: "Be then a wall of brass", "Learn to suffer", "Consider the end", "Go carefully", and "Pleasure Arises from Work".

And yet there is the familiar sense that all of this uprightness and all of this stubborn pride is only a mask, hiding the real truths and the real humanity. Thus, though Grandmother MacLeod claims that her family were the lairds of Morven and the constables of the Castle of Kinlochaline, the truth is that she "was born in Ontario, just like your Grandfather Connor, and her father was a horse doctor." In this way, it is clear that the characters dream dreams to avoid the truth. Their lives are full of a sense of 'what-might-have-been'. For example, Grandfather MacLeod made a great deal of money during his life, but his real passion was the reading of Greek plays in the original Greek. As Vanessa's father observed, "Maybe he would have liked to be a classical scholar - I don't know. But his father was a doctor, so that's what he was." Vanessa's father is similarly the victim of frustrated dreams. He confesses to Vanessa that when he was young he wanted to go into the merchant marine. His library, Vanessa learns, is testimony to the power of that vain dream:

> Seven-League Boots. Arabia Deserta. The Seven Pillars of Wisdom. Travels in Tibet. Count Lucknor the Sea Devil. And a hundred more. On a shelf by themselves were copies of the National Geographic magazine, which I looked at often enough, but never before with the puzzling compulsion which I felt now, as though I were on the verge of some discovery, something which I had to find out and yet did not want to know. I riffled through the picture-filled pages. Hibiscus and wild orchids grew in soft-petalled confusion. The Himalayas stood lofty as gods, with the morning sun on their peaks of snow. Leopards snarled from the vined depths of a thousand jungles. Schooners buffetted their white sails like the wings of giant angels against the great sea winds.

Accompanying the frustrated dreams is, again characteristically, the heavy sense of concealed guilt. Grandmother MacLeod suffers periodically from migraine headaches, the source of which is in part her continuing grief at the death of her younger son in the First War. Like Hagar, who did not solve her problem until the hour of her death, Grandmother MacLeod obviously favoured her younger son over Vanessa's father. That son, Roderick, had been with Ewen, Vanessa's father, in the trenches. Ewen clearly felt guilt at his own survival, and just as clearly Grandmother MacLeod had not come to terms with her grief over her dead son. In a manner typical of Manawaka families, this "skeleton in the closet" would not be banished; it would continue to haunt the family, for Grandmother MacLeod insists that the new child which is born be called Roderick.

The title of the story is obviously ironic. It expresses the kind of objective that motivates Grandmother MacLeod and her like. But, as even ten-year-old Vanessa realizes, it is not an expression of life as it really is. Human life is a series of paradoxes which are bewildering:

> I could not really comprehend these things, but I sensed their strangeness, their disarray. I felt that whatever God might love in this world, it was certainly not order.

"The Mask of the Bear" is an intriguing story which focuses on two main events: the end of Aunt Edna's love affair with Jimmy Lorimer and the death of Grandmother Connor. The bear of the title is, of course, Grandfather Connor, for the enormous winter coat he wore always is conceived by Vanessa as being symbolic of her grandfather's nature.

It is true that Mr. Connor showed only harshness. He was unspeakably rude to Jimmy Lorimer, whom Edna seemed to love deeply and genuinely. He was tyrannical with everyone in his household. He disregarded entirely the feelings of his wife, when she asked him before Lorimer's visit to be nice, for her sake. And yet, movingly, it is clear that the harshness and the gruffness were part of the mask that the old man wore to conceal his desperate need for tenderness:

> ... I saw one day in a museum the Bear Mask of the Haida Indians. It was a weird mask. The features were ugly and yet powerful. The mouth was turned down in an expression of sullen rage. The eyes were empty caverns, revealing nothing. Yet as I looked, they seemed to draw my own eyes towards them, until I imagined I could see somewhere within that darkness a look which I knew, a lurking bewilderment. I remembered then that in the days before it became a museum piece, the mask had concealed a man.

The view of human beings which emerges from this vision is

truly tragic. Locked within the self, unable to communicate on the deepest level with those around them, they hide behind their masks, bewildered by the passion of their emotions, knowing only the pain of regret when death visits.

Perhaps more poignantly than any of the stories, "A Bird in the House" communicates the feelings which death stirs in the living. Dr. MacLeod dies during a flu epidemic, and the MacLeod family, except for Grandmother MacLeod, who moves to Winnipeg, go to live in the Brick House of Grandfather Connor.

The poignancy comes in twelve-year-old Vanessa's apprehension of the sorrows that have been a part of her father's life. The insight begins in a conversation with her father on Remembrance Day, when she becomes aware of the hidden world of memories associated with his experiences in the First War. It is deepened by his cry of frustration and regret at the way his life has been shaped: "It's the damned house all the time. I haven't only taken on my father's house, I've taken on everything that goes with it, apparently." It is most vividly realized, years later, during the Second War, when Vanessa discovers a faded letter and a photograph in the drawers of her father's desk. The letter was obviously a love letter, and the photograph was obviously that of a French girl with whom her father had been in love. At that moment, Vanessa hoped that the girl had meant "some momentary and unexpected freedom" for her father.

Thus, the familiar, though nonetheless moving, theme returns: the inexorable entrapment of human beings, who are left sadly with the pain of their memories and regrets. Vanessa sees human beings as being like the sparrow which flies into her room, wanting freedom and frantically thrashing about with its wings in an effort to escape. The bird is freed; human beings are not.

In "The Loons", the main focus in upon Piquette Tonnerre, one of a family of French halfbreeds who lived in a squalid settlement just below Manawaka. Because Piquette was recovering from a tubercular hip, Dr. MacLeod invited her for a summer at the family cottage on Diamond Lake.

Belonging to one of the traditional Scots-Irish families of Manawaka, Vanessa did not know quite how to treat the surly and uncouth Piquette that summer. At first, Vanessa had the romantic notion that the girl, being half-Indian, could teach her all kinds of mysterious things about forest life, but Piquette's aggressive resistance to any warm relationship rendered that idea futile. When some of Vanessa's own friends arrived at the lake for their holiday, she ignored Piquette.

Vanessa did not see much of Piquette again until four years after Dr. MacLeod's death. Then, in the Regal Cafe, heavily made-up and dressed provocatively, Piquette revealed that she was going to be married to a city boy, an English fellow with "this real classy name", Alvin Gerald Cummings. The news confused Vanessa. Even as she mouthed the customary congratulations, she was thinking "how great her need must have been, that she had been forced to seek the very things she so bitterly rejected."

When Vanessa was eighteen, she went away to college. At the end of her first year, on a visit home, she asked her mother about Piquette. She was told that Piquette was dead. She had indeed married, but either her husband left her or she left him. She had returned with two small children to Manawaka, to live once more in her father's shack. She had become fat and slovenly and drunken. Finally, when a fire swept through the shack, she and her children had lost their lives.

The story, with Vanessa's reactions to Piquette as both a child and a woman, portrays the human tragedies that exist among ordinary folk in small towns. Cut off from respectable families, families like the Tonnerres drag out their days in pathetic degradation. The voice of their sorrow is, Vanessa realizes, the cry of the loons:

> No one can ever describe that ululating sound, the crying of the loons, and no one who has heard it can ever forget it. Plaintive, and yet with a quality of chilling mockery, those voices belonged to a world separated by aeons from our neat world of summer cottages and the lighted lamps of home.

The melancholy and the sadness of the cry were, after all, only of ephemeral interest to cottagers and the smug residents of respectable dwellings. In her life, Vanessa saw, Piquette knew the cry.

The central figure in "Horses of the Night" is Vanessa's cousin, Chris. He came to Manawaka at the age of fifteen to stay at the Brick House, so that he could finish his last three years of high school. There was no high school at Shallow Creek, where he lived.

Chris seemed to endure his sufferings and disappointments well. At the Brick House, he appeared to be able to ignore Grandfather Connor's grumblings at having another mouth to feed. Even later, when the Depression put an end to his hopes of university, Chris seemed to be able to approach life with optimism. He became a travelling salesman, though that was an endeavour doomed to failure because of the hard times. At last, he was forced to return to the family farm, since no jobs were to be had. Even there, when Vanessa visited Shallow Creek after her father's death, Chris seemed to be able to accept his disappointments well. However, when he joined the army and went to England, his mind finally surrendered. He was discharged because of mental problems and entered the provincial mental hospital, where he became completely passive.

Vanessa, who had felt close to Chris, realized at last both the source of his apparent ability to accept misfortune and the reason for his breakdown. He had survived by "distancing himself from the absolute unbearability of battle." As she thought of him now, living passively through the long days and nights, Vanessa's thoughts were sorrowful and tender:

> The night must move like this for him, slowly, all through the days and nights. I could not know whether the land he journeyed through was inhabited by terrors, the old monster-kings of the lake, or whether he had discovered at last a way for himself to make the necessary dream perpetual.

On the narrative level, "The Half-Husky" is the story of the dog that Vanessa got from Peter Chorniuk, the man who came from Galloping Mountain with Mr. Connor's supply of birchwood. Interwoven with the story of the dog is the story of Harvey Shinwell, who delivered the paper to the Connor household.

Harvey teased Nanuk, the dog, cruelly and unmercifully. He knew that he was safe in his malicious teasing, because Nanuk was confined to the yard. Distressed though she was, Vanessa could think of no solution to the problem. She had her revenge when Harvey stole a telescope which Roddie had left lying near the gate. Grandfather Connor marched wrathfully to the house of Harvey's aunt, with whom the boy lived, and recovered the stolen property. Thus, Vanessa had her revenge. Soon afterwards, Harvey began to work for an elderly Chinese who kept a cafe. About a year later, Harvey beat the owner severely and robbed him. Shinwell was caught quickly and jailed for six years.

The interest in the story lies in the parallel which is drawn between Harvey and the half-husky. Both were unwilling captives: the dog, wild by nature, was imprisoned in the yard; Harvey, an illegitimate child, was the prisoner of a squalid environment. Both, in the course of the story, reached physical maturity and increasingly sought to express their nature. Both were doomed creatures: Nanuk, too wild to be easily manageable, was put to death; Harvey disappeared from Vanessa's life also: "I never saw him again. I don't know where he went when he got out. Back in, I suppose."

"The Half-Husky" is an interesting story for its technique; it is also a moving story for the kind of human tragedy with which it deals. It is a reminder of grim aspects in the life of Manawaka. The Scots-Irish families reigned on in the comfort of their prosperity, armoured in their self-righteousness, but elsewhere in the town were others whom want and neglect stifled.

"Jericho's Brick Battlements" is the last story in the collection, and it is probably the closest to the themes enunciated in the novels. It deals, with contrapuntal rhythm, with the alternation between the sense of confinement and the need for escape. Edna Connor, pondering marriage to Wes Grigg, expresses the problem succinctly:

> ... I guess I've got used to being back here in the old dungeon. It's strange, Beth. Father's impossible, and certainly no one has said it oftener than I have. I have less patience with him than any of us has ever had, except possibly Vanessa, and she's only fourteen, for Heaven's sake. I know all that. But, he's - well, I guess it's just that I have the feeling that the *absolute* worst wouldn't happen here, ever. Things wouldn't actually fall apart. Do you know what I mean? We got through the Depression somehow. We never thought we would, but we did. I know it's more by good luck than good management. I'm perfectly aware of all that. And yet -

The problem was that Manawaka was more than a place in which people lived, that Grandfather Connor was more than an irascible old man, that the Brick House was more than a sheltering roof. Together, and combined with all the nuances of daily living, they were a way of life. As a way of life, it had its advantages, for it provided a sense of continuity, of security and of rightness. The misfortune was that it was not an environment in which human beings could live happily and grow and mature contentedly in the warmth of a shared love. From generation to generation, the process of entrapment continued. Grandmother Connor had been trapped in a marriage to an unlovable man. Aunt Edna for years had been trapped in loveless servitude in her father's house. Vanessa's mother, her freedom ended with the death of her husband, was obliged to return to her prison, taking up Edna's servitude when Edna left to be married.

Vanessa herself would succumb also, but she is saved by her mother, who obtains sufficient money to send her daughter to university. Yet there is irony in her escape. To begin with, it is accomplished, in part, with money given by Grandfather Connor. Moreover, visiting Manawaka twenty years later, Vanessa realizes that her escape can never be complete. True, the walls of Jericho seem to have fallen, for the old man is long since dead, and the Brick House, neglected and in disrepair, is the habitation of strangers. But a part of Grandfather Connor lives on in her, shaping her attitudes and framing her thoughts:

I parked the car beside the Brick House. The caragana hedge was unruly. No one had trimmed it properly that summer. The house had been lived in by strangers for a long time. I had not thought it would hurt me to see it in other hands, but it did. I wanted to tell them to trim their hedges, to repaint the window-frames, to pay heed to repairs. I had feared and fought the old man, yet he proclaimed himself in my veins.

A Bird in the House is an important part of Margaret Laurence's work as a writer. The stories, though published separately, belong together in one volume, for they portray an entire way of life that lies at the heart of the conflicts in the novels.

ESSAY QUESTIONS

1. Describe and explain the "crimes" for which Hagar Shipley felt herself to be responsible.

2. Analyze carefully ONE technique employed in the structure of *The Stone Angel.*

3. Explain the relevance of the title of the novel to the novel as a whole.

4. Give an account of (a) the Biblical imagery in the novel and (b) the flower imagery, emphasizing the relationship between the imagery and important themes.

5. Justify, by the use of coherent argumentation, the reading of a novel about a ninety-year-old woman by younger people.

6. Compare and contrast *The Stone Angel* and *The Fire-Dwellers,* emphasizing the element of guilt in both novels.

7. Compare and contrast Jason Currie (*The Stone Angel*) with Grandfather Connor (*A Bird in the House*).

8. Give an account of the Tonnerre family, using information from *The Stone Angel, The Fire-Dwellers* and *A Bird in the House.*

9. Compare and contrast Hagar Shipley with Vanessa MacLeod.

10. Write an essay on the use of irony in the works of Margaret Laurence.

11. Give an account of the values cherished by the prosperous inhabitants of Manawaka, explaining (a) the positive aspects of those values and (b) the destructive aspects of their values.